Siolence

Siolence

POETS ON WOMEN, VIOLENCE & SILENCE

Edited by
SUSAN MCMASTER

❧ ❦

Art work by
MARIE ELYSE ST. GEORGE
and HEATHER SPEARS

The essays in *Siolence: Poets on Women, Violence and Silence* are drawn from the panels and presentations of the Feminist Caucus of the League of Canadian Poets between 1982 and 1995, published as separate chapbooks for each year as part of the *Living Archives* series. The writings in this volume are drawn, in part, from the following chapbooks: *Silences* (1992), *Women and Violence* (1992), and *What Is a Nice Feminist . . . ?* (1993). Two forthcoming volumes — *Reinventing Memory: Poets on Women and Language,* and *Binary Opposition: The Sexual Politics of Poetry* — will complete the collected essays from this decade of literary feminism in Canadian poetry.

Poems and essays in *Siolence* (sometimes in other versions) have appeared as follows, and are reprinted by permission of the authors and publishers:

"Silences longer than we can bear," by John Barton, in *Poetry Canada* (Vol. 13, No. 1, and "Undercurrent," in *Capilano Review* (1994).

"I Write Imaginary Stories," by Ayanna Black, in *Voices: 16 Canadian Writers of African Descent* (Toronto: HarperPerennial, 1992).

"there are no words . . ." and "how long does it take . . .," by Di Brandt, in her *Jerusalem, beloved* (Winnipeg: Turnstone Press, 1995).

"Rhéaume," by Richard Harrison, in his *Hero of the Play* (Toronto: Wolsak & Wynn, 1994); and "The Silence in *Iron John,*" *Poetry Canada* (Vol. 15, No. 2).

"Siolence" by Penn Kemp, in *Paragraph* (Summer 1993) and *Poetry Canada* (Vol. 15, no. 2). First presented as a talk in the Humber College Silver Anniversary Speakers' Series in 1992.

"Women and Violence: Another, Mother, Way," by Susan McMaster, *Motherworks* (Spring 1995).

"The Acts, number 7," by Erin Mouré, *Furious* (Toronto: Anansi, 1988).

"The Woman in the Wall," by Sandra Nicholls, *Woman of Sticks, Woman of Stones* (Kingston: Quarry Poetry Books, 1998).

The publisher acknowledges the support of The Canada Council for the Arts and the Department of Canadian Heritage for the arts of writing and publishing in Canada.

ISBN 1-55082-158-x

Front cover: *Eve's Choice*, for wisdom with risk, by Marie Elyse St. George, is reproduced by permission of the artist. First reproduced in *Voices*, by Marie Elyse St. George and Anne Szumigalski (Regina: Coteau Books, and Saskatoon: Mendel Art Gallery, 1995).

Interior illustrations: Sketches from panel presentations of the Feminist Caucus of the League of Canadian Poets, graphite on paper, by Heather Spears.

Design by Susan Hannah.

Printed and bound in Canada by AGMV/Marquis, Cap-St-Ignace, Quebec.

Published by Quarry Press Inc., P.O. Box 1061, Kingston, Ontario K7L 4Y5 Canada
www.quarrypress.com

Contents

Foreword

❦ ❦

Siolence, the title of this collection, is a word coined by Penn Kemp to encapsulate the blending that so often occurs between violence and the silence enabling it.

For more than a decade, a group of feminist writers in the League of Canadian Poets, self-dubbed the Feminist Caucus, have been gathering once a year at the League's annual meetings to wrestle with issues of language and gender, to share revelations and convictions and poems, to gain strength to guide them in their next year's work, and to reaffirm their place in the community of people who spend much of their lives working to end the violence of language and the silencing of voices that corrupt our society.

These gatherings have two main elements. The first is a panel and discussion, the topics ranging widely across areas of gender and voice. Speakers are limited to five-minute presentations and no poetry, though they often break both rules; but a result of the restrictions has been a passionate compression in the resulting texts, an elision and implication as well as a no-nonsense plain speaking, that have proved remarkably provocative. The precise and powerful use of language that characterizes these presentations may also come from the fact that the speakers are all poets — writers who specialize in making every word count. The discussion that follows each panel is always lively; often it erupts into vigorous argument. Sometimes — I remember this happening at the "violence" panel in 1992 — it deepens into a quiet, intense, and compassionate sharing that moves everyone present. The most exciting hour of the weekend, possibly even the year, for some, is the second part of the gathering — an open reading, with one poem offered by each person present. In these pieces, we share our ideas and insights in the form we know best.

The effects reach far beyond a few days. Into articles, letters, phone calls, private and public wrangles in columns like the one in the League newsletter, first called "The Woman I Am" (after Dorothy Livesay's book of that name) and then "Feminist Letters." One of the more interesting exchanges is a collection of letters called *Two Women Talking* between Bronwen Wallace and Erin Mouré, outstanding poets and organizers of the first Caucus meetings. Not surprisingly, the central concern of the *Living Archives* series is language and gender issues. Men who turn a (com)passionate focus on these issues are welcome in the Caucus, at the readings and on the panels.

In fact, so powerful are these events that, not many years after the panels began, members of the Feminist Caucus began talking about collecting the texts into a permanent form. The *Living Archives* series of chapbooks, now in its eleventh volume, includes the original panel texts plus essays, poems, revisions, and additions. The chapbooks are enriched by a remarkable series of "Body Windows" drawings by Marie Elyse St. George and by vivid and often humorous sketches of the speakers in full spate by Heather Spears. Both artists have kindly allowed their work to be used to illustrate the current collection.

As the *Living Archives* series grew, the texts began to rebound off each other, talk to each other. The decisive moment for the current volume occurred when Quarry editor Bob Hilderley realized that the neologism "siolence" not only described a world of experience, but drew a number of essays from the series together in a telling way. Quarry offered to publish the first of a proposed set of three collections which will make these years of thought and writing more widely available. And here we are.

Several points are worthy of note. For those not familiar with Canadian poetry, the *Living Archives* series and *Siolence* present the work of poets honored both in Canada and abroad. Artist Marie Elyse St. George's recent book with poet Anne Szumigalski won the 1995 Governor General's award for poetry, Canada's top literary honor; other Governor General award winners in this volume are Erin Mouré and Heather Spears, while both Di Brandt and Dan Moses have been nominated. Di is also a winner of the prestigious CBC Literary Prize, as are Nadine McInnis and Heather Spears. The National Magazine Awards, the Pat Lowther and Gerald Lampert Awards, the Dillon Commonwealth Prize, the National Poetry Award, the Canadian Authors' Association prizes, the Patricia Hackett Award (Australia), the Short Grain, the Leacock, the Lampman, the Acorn, the Jordan . . . authors in this collection have garnered a notable collection of national and international accolades.

More important, each of the writers represented here has written one or more fine books of poetry. These are often ground-breaking books, books that shake the tree of poetry to knock down strange and exotic fruit. Not surprisingly, the sensibility of risk also sings through the prose the poets offer in this collection. In fact, so intense are the essays — and so enhanced by the occasional poems included (against the rules!) in the original chapbooks — that I requested poems from all the writers in *Siolence* for this collection. The poems extend the range of discussion and offer an invigorating taste of the remarkable writing being produced by feminist and gay poets today.

The texts in *Siolence* are drawn largely from the two volumes *Silences* and *Women and Violence*. Following my introductory notes are excerpts from the original introductions to each volume, by their respective editors, Sarah Klassen and Erin Mouré. Two essays from *What Is a Nice Feminist . . . ?* are also included, the thoughtful "Writing with Your Clothes Off," by Sandra Nicholls, and "Writing the Unspeakable: No Rules, No Precedents" by Libby Zoë Oughton, which appropriately ends the book with a gripping account of a feminist publisher, a terrified author, and a long-silenced story about to explode into print.

— *Susan McMaster*

Violence

SARAH KLASSEN

Sarah Klassen is a Winnipeg writer who has published four collections of poetry: *Borderwatch* (Netherlandic Press); *Violence and Mercy* (Netherlandic Press); nominated for the Pat Lowther Award and the McNally Robinson best book of the year award; *Journey to Yalta* (Turnstone Press), which received the Gerald Lampert Memorial Award; and *Dangerous Elements* (Quarry Press). She won the First Short Grain Contest in 1989. Her work has been anthologized in *Liars and Rascals* (University of Waterloo Press), *Out of Place* (Coteau), *Acts of Concealment: Mennonite/s Writing in Canada* (University of Waterloo Press), and *Postcards: New Canadian Fiction*, edited by Kristina Russello (Black Moss Press). Her work has been featured with musical accompaniment in performances of *Singing at the Fire: Voices of Anabaptist Martyrs* and *Born Again: A Song Cycle of Our Time*.

Violence

※ ※

In a violent world we long for peace. We want an end to war and oppression, an end both to physical brutality that destroys the body and to the more subtle but no less cruel abuses that victimize the dispossessed. We believe we must speak and take action against those who destroy the spirits of women, children, and all those individuals and groups who in our society have not been empowered with dignity and worth. We want a better world for us all.

"We" in this case are feminist writers, poets, who are horrified by abuse and are sometimes the victims of it. At times it threatens to immobilize us and put an end to writing. At other times we throw ourselves with so much zeal and anger into the cause of justice that we have no time or energy for our work.

Most often we find ourselves somewhere between these two extremes, perhaps transforming the raw material violence provides us with into poems and other forms of art. How many of us, for instance, responded to the Montreal massacre, the Westray mine disaster, or the Bernardo murder trial by writing, or at least thinking about writing, a poem?

Opposing violence can be a risky business, no question. How can we confront violence and undertake vigorous action against it without becoming violent ourselves? In one of the texts in this collection the writer quotes her mother, who warned her: "Learn to forgive, for you become what you hate." There is risk involved when our words, our poems, name the violence that others prefer to leave unspoken. Another contributor describes unscrupulous attempts to use her own words against her.

In my letter to the original panelists, I phrased the topic, at first formulated simply as "Women and Violence," to include the word "reconciliation." In doing this I may have manipulated the focus; if so, it happened because of my own background, growing up as a Mennonite in one of the historic peace churches. I was surprised, later, to learn that several of the panelists had similar connections. Maja Bannerman and Susan McMaster come from the Religious Society of Friends (Quakers), and Di Brandt from a traditional Mennonite community. Nadine McInnis and Brenda Niskala added their voices in further exploration of the topic. Each writer approached the issue of violence from her own experience and perspective.

Afua Cooper, moderator of the original panel, generously gave all the time to the speakers, and so you will not read a statement from her. I remember how she invited us into silence before introducing the speakers, making a quiet space, a sort of separate peace, in the midst of a busy conference schedule. This small interlude was an appropriate preparation both for the speaking and the listening, and also for the discussion that followed.

Responses from listeners ranged from frustration to cool-headed, practical suggestions; from outrage at power systems to a reflection on the violence inside; from faith in nonviolent methods to a questioning of their effectiveness.

I invite you to enter the following pages and join the discussion, where writers express their horror at violence and their yearning for a better world, and where they envision their words becoming the powerful tools needed to help forge it.

(from the Introduction to the chapbook
Women and Violence, Feminist Caucus,
League of Canadian Poets)

TRIBUTE

February 1997

The same morning I'm reading *God will wipe away*
every tear from their eyes the BBC says Deng
Xiaoping is dead. I smile remembering that creased face
that rotund tranquil smile. Deng standing small and solid
with Richard Nixon, Mikhail Gorbachev. At Tienamen
his presence was invisible but potent as those tanks that rolled in,
rolled over insubordination, crushed limbs of the young
the way a cruel hand might break the delicate stems of flowers.

That day the mothers' outcry overshadowed birdsong,
out-wailed the guns. Their eyes were blinded with those tears
God promises to wipe away
along with hunger, thirst, the cruel noon-day sun
beating without a trace of bias on the traveller still far
from any destination, the potato harvest, a solitary child
building castles in a sandpile, a family picnic in the park.

The sun warmed Deng Xiaoping when he was still alive. Smiling.
Rain, also, falls alike on old and young, on murderers, heart-broken mothers,
its soothing touch a respite from the heat, a hindrance to the picnic
and the harvest. (A girl at school, I understood a storm was expected
the day the innocent doctor in *Macbeth* said: *God,*
God forgive us all.)

Silence

ERIN MOURÉ

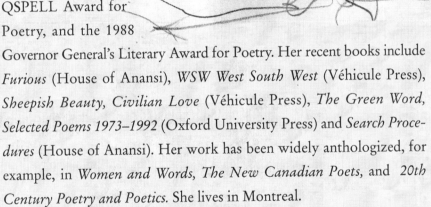

Erin Mouré is the author of seven poetry collections and the winner of two National Magazine Awards for Poetry, the 1985 Pat Lowther Memorial Award, the 1990 QSPELL Award for Poetry, and the 1988 Governor General's Literary Award for Poetry. Her recent books include *Furious* (House of Anansi), *WSW West South West* (Véhicule Press), *Sheepish Beauty, Civilian Love* (Véhicule Press), *The Green Word, Selected Poems 1973–1992* (Oxford University Press) and *Search Procedures* (House of Anansi). Her work has been widely anthologized, for example, in *Women and Words, The New Canadian Poets,* and *20th Century Poetry and Poetics*. She lives in Montreal.

Silence

❧ ❦

Silence. It's something that I confronted most directly in *Furious*. The act of speaking and writing is always a coming out of silence in a way, although, as some of the writers in this collection point out, you can never leave silence behind. For me, at the same time you speak an image, you are cancelling out other images; at the same time you're telling a story one way you are cancelling out other possible ways of telling the story. Or you could be.

Maybe the structure of meaning itself is a structure of silence, which doesn't say that meaning is rigid but just that it can be problematic. So it is interesting here to have so many different voices taking their own tack on the issue of silence. The view they offer us is much more than the sum of the parts.

A couple of writers have chosen to address "issues" where the manufacture and imposition of silence is ongoing, subtle, and pernicious, instead of focussing on their personal experience of silencing. I could put Richard Harrison most directly into this category, but John Barton also addresses a wider and ongoing silence, one that extends into the fabric of the law.

Two other essayists talk about silence in a kind of "compositional" way. Daniel David Moses's piece considers silence as contrast rather than as somebody shutting somebody else up — a conflictual thing. As well, he does address silence as an issue with political implications: as in, when you are called to speak, people have expectations of you as a representative of a community, and in the end, your speech is only that of an individual. And how could it be otherwise?

Penn Kemp also writes about composition, and the silences embedded for years in our heads about violence toward women within the walls of the family, so embedded that it is extremely difficult for the woman enduring violence to acknowledge, admit, know what it is she is undergoing. Penn coins the term "siolence" to show the close links between the silence and the violence, and talks about the compositional and political consequences of writing of these matters, especially a few years ago.

Then we have our mystery contestant, Ayanna Black, who, as we'll see, felt silenced by the instructions originally given to panelists to stay away from poetry, the form that best bears her voice outward. Fortunately, she disobeys and alters the instruction! And she does speak.

I'll end by quoting from a poem of my own from *Furious,* at a point where I talk about silence, because it ends with the idea of civic memory, of memory as a communal thing, and the idea that we have to find our way to speak in it. Otherwise just the traditional dominant voices speak.

(from the Introduction to the chapbook
Silences, Feminist Caucus,
League of Canadian Poets)

⚜ ⚜

THE ACTS, NUMBER 7

What is key to this desire: To have one's existence affirmed by others. Or, put oneself at risk forever (a panic at the cell's edge). Or is it affirmation, first, that then makes the risk possible? To bear it. The risk of, kissing her.

The embrace first, then the utterance.

What this need for affirmation meant before was having an existence affirmed by men. Knowing how they praise well what affirms their relation. They do not have to put them-selves at risk, which women have always had to do, to exist, to speak, to have their existence affirmed by others.

What I had not spoken! The way she cried out because of my silence, and how I chose it, stubborn. My defense of necessity. Because my eyes and my whole body could see that the words and bodies of women were not listened to or affirmed.

But we women listen so carefully to each other. The resurrection of the woman's body is of Kore, not the phallic king-dom. This affirmation is the true necessity. To inhabit freely the civic house of memory I am kept out of.

Oh!

Siolence

PENN KEMP

Penn Kemp was born and raised near London, Ontario. Having taught creative writing in Ontario schools since 1966, she has completed a Master of Eduction in Creativity at O.I.S.E. in Toronto; her thesis is a book on writing for teachers called *What Springs to Mind*. She continues to give writing and sound workshops across the continent, often as writer-in-residence (Labrador, Victoria, New York State, and recently at a women's university in Bombay). Best known as an innovative sound poet, she is also a playwright and novelist with fifteen books to her credit. The play *What the Ear Hears Last* was recently performed at Theatre Passe Muraille in Toronto. She performs with the jazz group HandSlang and records audiotapes, including *Epiphanies* with David Prentice on flute (Glenn Gould Studio, Toronto), *Tranceform* (Audiographics, New York City), and *Ear Rings* (Underwhich, Toronto).

Siolence

❧ ❦

In her biography of Elizabeth Smart, Rosemary Sullivan writes: "Every witness leaves gaps, deliberate or not. A biographer learns to listen between the words for the potent silences." She describes how Elizabeth's sister, cutting out some of the information in material she was sending, left Rosemary to wonder at that gap with a cryptic note: "Eat your heart out."

But what if the biography is one's own memoir? One's own mind is then the site of potent silences to be examined: Mind the Gap. As Erin Mouré has said, the work is to decipher that anxiety, not to smooth it over too soon or to bury it.

Silence for me has been the background upon which my writing is figure. Writing is the arabesque back to recover what has been lost. Semi-autobiographical fiction gives me permission to speak the obvious mysteries.

Robert Bly describes a similar gap in his early book, appropriately called *The Silence of Snowy Fields,* as the denial of his father's drinking. The gap is a wound for Bly – for me as woman that wound is womb, nest and family.

In the late seventies I wrote a novel, *Falling Towers,* which was shortlisted for the Seal Book Award, but never published. Now I understand why. In it, I could only deal obliquely with the topic of family violence and its effect on children. The cares and the fears were still too fresh for me to deal directly with this topic. There was a gap in the writing, a gulf in my consciousness that could not yet be leaped. It is only now that I have written the introductory pages which make sense of the rest of the novel, from which I excerpt:

His fingers closed, blunt tips touching, the heels of the palms meeting, almost as in prayer. The hands ringing her throat, gold wedding ring pressing into her gullet. Even now, her body responded to the closeness of him, still dearly familiar and almost real. But she herself had already disappeared up the smoky trail, out the top of her head into the wide blue sky. Up there was a buzzing as of bees in the air, in the cool expanse. And a strange croak that seemed to have begun in her throat and travelled up with her into the wind. It was a croak; she was flying. She was a gull and free. Mewing, she hovered, opened her new eyes to glimpse the roof of their house, of all the houses, so puny from this height. They were five rows of little boxes nestled in a protective, billowing grove of trees along one edge of the Island. Beyond them, around her, the water sparkled, waiting, eternal.

Violent shaking startled her out of freedom: a sudden updraft, had she flown into a hurricane? She was being pulled back, down the vortex into a body she thought she had surrendered. The sound was in her ear, a roaring, carol, carol, but she heard no song. Nothing but Phil's voice, loud as Poseidon in a seashell. She swam now in an ocean of blood. Swirling red currents filled every cranny of her consciousness and this time she went under.

Cause and effect; events and who knew for sure what did happen. When she returned, the room was empty again but it too was swirling around her. It was an ordinary Island living room, filled with the brightly coloured booty of past travels: hangings and curtains and rugs. But now the Turkish reds and oranges, the Moroccan blacks of curtain danced a jig of molecules that confused her senses. She was lying on the couch, the one real piece of furniture they owned. At least it was steady. She shut her eyes again. She would not see.

She heard his footsteps, running closer. Water, soaking her head. She looked at him. A yellow cast of fear lay over the last red flare of rage on his face. But the hands that held the basin barely trembled. "If you've quite recovered," Phil declared, "I'll head off to the city. Just take it easy, Carole. Is there anything we need? You'll be all right."

Irony of statement, concern or relief: it didn't matter. The pain nearly divided her head from her shoulders. "I'll be all right," she attempted re-entry. "Just go." Instead, her voice croaked. The words and the ability to make words had disappeared. And Phil was already out the door. A flash of his yellow bike, and silence, except for the buzzing of wasps in her head.

What had it been about this time? How long? Could either of them remember? There was a complicity between them: nothing had happened. They could talk to no-one, certainly not each other, about the sudden black holes, the mine fields in ordinary conversation that would suddenly erupt. Because most of the time, they were not there. The house was simply a house, the scene domestic, cats and kids and cauliflower on the stove. Carole could talk to no-one. She could not talk. When she tried, once, twice, her father reminded her of family pride, her friends reminded her their business was not to interfere. Not to know.

And where could she go anyway, on her own with two kids and no money and a body that would not move. Guilt, shame, Carole wrapped those qualities around her to keep warm, as if they were her own, protecting her from the eyes of neighbours, hiding the black and yellowing bruises under sleeves and stockings. What had she done? The dishes, drying in the sink. What had he done?

His fingers she had studied so closely, bald sentinels drumming up action. Beating to their own rhythm, the jazz that syncopated his every movement.

Next time. No, there would be no next time. There was never going to be a next time. This Carole believed on faith. This Phil believed on faith. When he returned that night after the children were asleep, Phil knew of course that he had changed, knew his rage had disappeared forever, as if it never was. Carole knew there was no such thing as fear. They held onto each other all night. Without a word.

That story of violence was muffled because in the framework of the seventies it was not acknowledged to exist. That story I could not tell, because, as ground dissolves to figure, it did not exist in the positive noise of ordinary living. The action of violence upon articulation might best be expressed in a neologism: *siolence*.

Even in introducing a later book, *Binding Twine,* about losing custody of my children, I could not be direct. The blame, along with the mantle of silence, I still took on as my own. The root cause of violence I slipped in askance, in the middle of the foreword, where it might not be noticed:

> This is the testimony the judge did not, could not hear . . . I have allowed myself to be victimized. I have learned. I do not allow myself to be victimized now. I take immediate action. I let nothing slip by. The central issue is passivity: how to break through the pattern of resignation, the sense of defeat and loss.
>
> For years I lived in a state of shock, driven out of my body. Yes, my pelvis split at the birth of each child. Yes, I was beaten and had nowhere to go. The effect was I could not grasp reality easily. I saw things as if I were a foot above myself, hands at the ends of long poles, ineffectual. Now, having worked through the terror, I am here, present, willing to face what comes. Willing to let this book out in the hope that it reaches others who have been where I have.
>
> One women's account to every woman, every person.

Shell-shocked. This is the gap into which I stuffed the memories I could not accept as real: eighteen months of clinging by a silent scream to life in a familial war zone. The body has a long memory and hides its fear long after it knows it should feel safe. I'm a writer and not easily squelched, and yet I was silenced for twenty years, by fear, by shame. Violence stuns; the mouth opens and after a while no scream emerges.

What can the experience of *siolence* be like for those who do not turn to language easily? As we find our own tongues, in turn we need to listen to others who are beginning to tell their stories. Encouragement is a safe place, a silence that is attentive and welcoming, so that all our stories may be heard. *Let those bones speak.*

Those of us who have experienced *siolence* recognize one another. There is a certain look in the eye (I first wrote eve). A gingerness, as if we are still afraid to touch down. I prepare this piece at an adult education centre, while waiting to receive individual writers.

Like calls to like.

The woman who hesitantly shows me her poem has written about gathering lovely flowers, red and blue, making the house beautiful once more with their scent. Her words describing the meadow are so light and airy that they feel unreal. To ground the writing, I ask her what might be behind the fantasy. "I had to escape," she tells me and the story she has never told pours out. "He beat on me. I could take that. But once he laid a hand on the kids, I got us out. I ran without a word." And came back to school. Stories swirl in our wake, till I am whisked off to the next class. She decides to write what happened in her marriage as her "Independent Study."

Painting

Hands on hip
this woman looks so-
lid. Emp-
ty. Light streams

body's dispersal.
Flashes off solar
plex-
us.

Vast night sky. Burnt
umber pushes
her head past her eyes.

Anguish wished far
far. Wide spread
legs. Ecstasy on-
going.

Light so light and
lovely. Who though's
ready for this
final dis/

    solution?

I Write / I Write Imaginary / Stories

AYANNA BLACK

Ayanna Black was born in Jamaica and lived in England before immigrating to Canada in 1964. Her poetry has been anthologized in various books such as *Sp/ELLes, Women and Words, Other Voices, One Out of Many,* and *Daughters of the Sun, Women of the Moon.* Her nonfiction writings have appeared in *Fuse* magazine, *West Coast Line, Fireweed,* and *The Best Writing on Writing* (Story Press). She is one of the founding members *Tiger Lily,* Canada's first magazine by women of color. She's author of the poetry collections *No Contingencies* (Williams/Wallace) and co-author of *Linked Alive* (Éditions Trois). Black is editor of two collections of poetry and non-fiction, *Voices: 16 Canadian Writers of African Descent* (HarperPerennial) and *Fiery Spirits* (HarperCollins). She has read and conducted poetry workshops in public schools, universities, libraries, and art galleries in Canada, the United Kingdom, the United States, and Italy. She lives in Toronto.

I Write / I Write Imaginary / Stories

❧ ❧

I must admit I had a difficult time working with the outline for this presentation. The outline stipulated "no poetry . . . don't read poetry." Frankly, I had a hard time accepting this; after all, I'm a poet, what else? I felt the outline was yet another layer of silence, and definitely undercut what the Feminist Caucus is attempting to achieve. Consequently, I had a difficult time thinking what I could write and what I wanted from this particular topic. But, thinking through the absence of my biological father, I felt that the topic had some relevance and could be contextualized to form the framework for this paper.

When I finally decided that I must write on Silence, I still had a laborious time because I wanted to write about it from a personal point of view. I had an initial idea, then many ideas, but couldn't hold onto any one concretely. I was getting confused and frustrated until I remembered "A Village in My Head," a short story by Makeda Silvera. It is about a woman writer wanting to tell her own story, but the women villagers want her to tell their story instead. To put Silvera's tale into context, it is an issue of community responsibility versus the individual crossing boundaries.

However, I came to the realization that the ideas occurring to me were the voices of my ancestors, telling me to re-examine the meaning of silence on a wider spectrum. And that I had to do them – my ancestors – justice. I had to include their voices as part of my history. My ancestors were telling me that I couldn't write just from my personal experience. I had instead to go back to a historical framework. This ended my confusion.

As soon as she saw me she gave a loud shriek, and also ran into my arms. I was quite overpowered: neither of us could speak; but for a considerable time, clung to each other in mutual embraces, unable to do anything but weep.¹

Don't let her speak! gasped half a dozen in her ear. She moved slowly and solemnly to the front, laid her bonnet at her feet, and turned her great speaking eyes to me. There was a great hissing sound of disapprobation above and below. I rose, announced, "Sojourner Truth," and begged the audience to keep silent for a few minutes.²

Silence (vt) silenced, silencing. 1: to compel or reduce to silence; still. 2: to restrain from expression; suppress. 3: to cause, to cease hostile firing or criticism.³

Historically, my ancestors were involuntarily taken from Africa and transported to various parts of the New World. Some worked on plantations; some were auctioned and some killed. They had no choice . . . held at gun point . . . what could they have done? Their communities being ravaged . . . languages being demolished. Silenced.

Most Western historians have not been willing to admit that there is an African history to be written about and that this history predates the emergence of Europe by thousands of years. It is not possible for the World to have waited in darkness for the Europeans to bring the light because, for the most of the early history of man, the Europeans themselves were in darkness. When the lights of culture came for the first time to the people who would later call themselves Europeans, it came from Africa and Middle Eastern Asia. Most history books tend to deny or ignore this fact.⁴

In the New World, for People of African Descent, histories were whitened out in books and the education systems, were written of and spoken by other writers or people who considered themselves to be experts in *their* construction of what they called "ethnicity."

Africans in the New World are themselves implicated in the terrible silence at the heart of the crime of the New World African slavery. In our urge to put the past behind us, we have often turned our thoughts away from this event to our history. Knowing that we have always been more than slaves, we have been reluctant to have our children taught about slavery. And quite rightly so, if that is the only aspect of our history taught to us: it would only serve to reinforce images of negativity that already exist in the culture, particularly if taught insensitively or badly. The avoidance is understandable but dangerous, both for us and for the non-African population which has very little knowledge or understanding of the crime carried out against Africans.[5]

For me, this crime was the infrastructure silencing People of African Descent, and which continues even today. Silences, for me, are a synthesis of journeys through my ancestral histories, including the patriarchal realities and values, a synthesis which enables me to gain a theoretical point of view, helps me interface with my conflicts of silence, and thus speak a language with clarity and substance.

If I am not myself, who will be for me?
And if I am only for myself, what am I?
And if not now, when?[6]

Personally, it is very difficult to separate the acts of psychological silence and mental violence from the act of forgetting. They are interrelated. And if I separate them, I would then believe that I was developing a schizophrenic personality. When a society does not represent or give access to certain groups or individuals, and when they are spoken for by people who cannot comprehend their pain or understand their icons, imageries, and words (which are often excluded from the system), this presents a framework to foster silencing. It internalizes rage, which can be acted out in many forms: pent-up energy, insecurity, etc. Silence and rage are co-habitants. Living in the same environment. Hidden. Often hidden in the body. But they can charge like a lioness in search of food . . . at anyone, anywhere, anytime. Silence is often rooted in rejection, deprivation, lack of access, and betrayal. How did my ancestors break out of their silences and how did they behave?

. . . they continued to create. in spite of jim crow. in spite of lynchings. in spite of laws against them speaking their tongues, playing their drums – in spite of the rules against their religion. in spite of; in spite of in spite. they creating. the only new musical form to come out of the new world – jazz. they creating. reggae, rap and funk; they creating calypso. in spite of. the blues of bessie, and billy and big mama thorton. in spite of. they creating.[7]

This was one way of breaking their silence. I'm grateful for it, because it is part of the legacy which I have inherited. And even today, this is a continuum for African People in the New World.

The power of the imagination is so great, it can actually do and create anything we need for survival, psychologically and physically.

I grew up without my biological father. I never met him. He left Jamaica before I was born. But he kept up his responsibilities. My Uncle P, as I called him then and even do today, was my male role model. As a girl growing up, the only girl without a father among my peer group, I invented my father. And I told my friends all kinds of adventurous stories about him and kept them up-to-date as to his whereabouts. Over the years, these stories became well rooted into my psyche, to some extent became a part of my life. They were lies, of course, but they gave me a voice, a voice regarding daughter-father relationships, and actually created a space where I belonged.

It was years later that I discovered that he was pushing himself through my writings. And that I had to reclaim him finally. Reclaim all aspects of that which I had blocked out. Although I recognized that I was breaking the silence in my earlier work, I'm grateful to the process of writing this paper. I have gained some perspective on my conflicts. And this is the first time that I have written about them in a conscious manner. In prose. This prose format. In previous works, it has always been creative . . . the poetics. In concluding, although I was told no poems. I will share with you one of my poems that exemplifies the breaking of my silence.

1. "The Life of Gustavus Vassa," in *The Classic Slave Narratives*, edited by Henry Louis Gates (New York: New American Library, 1987).

2. Angela Yvonne Davis, *Women, Race, and Class* (New York: Random House, 1981).

3. *Webster's Ninth New Collegiate Dictionary* (Springfield, MA: Merriam-Webster, 1987).

4. John Henrick Clarke, "Introduction," in *Introduction to African Civilization*, edited by John G. Jackson (Secusus, NJ: Citadel Press, 1970).

5. Marlene Nourbese Philip, *Showing Grit: Showboating North of the 44th Parallel* (Toronto: Poui Publications, 1993).

6. Marlene Nourbese Philip, *Showing Grit*.

7. Marlene Norbese Philip, *Showing Grit*.

⊰⊱ ⊰⊱

1. seed

going it alone was never my ambition
I knew at 13 yrs old
I knew
I knew it was
not fashionable like the contents of *Vogue*
today she writes she's going it alone –
single motherhood by   choice
or despair? the sperm bank is her obsession
and seduction
technicalizing the perfect seed for sprouting

what about the history?
smelling father's odour   smell touch and touch
like my cat Zwardi mews and mews and cuddles
in my lap for my smell   my body contact

2. cloud

I never learned fatherly games
like my friends Carol Nerissa Pauline
when the pains was
too much for my body
to resist   I fell
in love with his absence   seven years old
and buried him over and over
his glass casket covered
with white purple black
clouds
I write
I write imaginary
stories

3. rain

black hole
this is not your crude joke
this is a celestial reality
emptiness longings
my grandma agnes knew:
she fills me
with old photographs   him holding
        me   six months old   him feeding
me   him feeding feeding   photographs
photographs and letters and words
I cannot read words that make rain
drops I hear the sound
of raindrops I don't need raindrops
too much pain, too much
grandma agnes howling sound level
with wind I'm inside
the sun his voice the healer
his face a sun
flower

4. feminism

he says feminism is not our problem
not for us it's dividing the race
I say I'm piecing
my world together already divided
before me years ago
divided
she sits regal
passionately pushing the right keys
re: feminism interspersing
her attitudes re: men
this is my centre   centre
my politics calling upon
within my healer   my survival
I write stories
I write

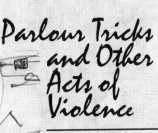

Parlour Tricks and Other Acts of Violence

BRENDA NISKALA

Brenda Niskala, a poet and fiction writer from the Coteau Hills of central Saskatchewan, has worked as a crisis counsellor, bush plane lawyer, writer-in-residence (North Battleford), branch representative for ACTRA, and co-executive director for the Saskatchewan Publishers Group. Her poetry has been published in the collection *Ambergris Moon* (Thistledown) and the anthologies *Lodestone* (Fifth House), *Dancing Visions* (Thistledown), *Heading Out* (Coteau), *What Is Already Known* (Thistledown), *Sky High* (Coteau), and *Bridges 4* (Prentice Hall). She has served on the editorial boards of *Grain, Briarpatch, NeWest Review,* and Coteau Books, and represented writers on the Canadian Reprography Collective (CanCopy), the Minister's Advisory Committee for the Status of the Artist in Saskatchewan, the Film/Video Professional Development Coordinating Committee and the Regina Arts Commission. Brenda has given readings and creative writing workshops at the University of Regina and the Sage Hill Writing Experience and in schools and libraries across the province. She has also served as the Saskatchewan Writers Guild Electronic-Writer-in-Residence.

Parlour Tricks and Other Acts of Violence

⚜ ⚜

You push pins through my flesh at a party
pressing silver through skin
everyone knows
with tricks
the pleasure is all in the audience
in the stillness and the pain
no one mentions

— Kim Morrissey, *Poems for Men Who Dream of Lolita*
(Coteau, 1992)

The subject is violence. It might as well be love. It's that broad. And it's that basic. Violence is the absence of love. Not that people committing violent acts are unloved, not that they love too little. During acts of violence love is forgotten. Other things flood in. Self-loathing. Jealousy. Impatience. Anger. Sometimes hate.

And sometimes not feeling at all, except a curiosity, a dullness, a forgetting. The absence of feeling, but especially the absence of love.

So how do I know? I have committed acts of violence. At least in my mind. I have recreated acts of violence dozens of times, through the eyes of my clients, as a defence lawyer in the criminal justice system. And, yes, I have been the victim of violence. I don't want to talk about that.

I want to talk about a town in northern Saskatchewan: La Loche, population 1800. It boasted the highest birth rate per capita in the world in 1981, and is accessible by roads only because of the Key Lake uranium mine forty kilometres north of the town. When I worked there in the mid-1980s, it had 99% unemployment, the highest rate of incarceration per capita in Saskatchewan, and the highest rate of violent crime.

La Loche was never supposed to be a town. The Dene and Métis people living there were moved to the site, to make way for development. Never mind that the lake they were moved to cannot sustain them. That the trap lines are disrupted by oil drilling activity. That there is no economic base.

I was in town once when the edge started crumbling. In Los Angeles or on Yonge Street they'd call it a riot. In La Loche, for a particular portion of the population, it was just another day of hanging around until they closed the Liquor Board store. La Loche has the dubious distinction of being the only place in Saskatchewan, and one of only a handful in Canada, where the RCMP can close the Liquor Board store at any time they see fit. And they do. But if their timing is a bit off, this friendly town becomes angry.

The problem in La Loche is not the individuals, the particular batterers and murderers, the mundane or bizarre details of their acts. The problem is structural.

Violence is embedded in this, in our society.

I've worked as a crisis counsellor, in women's shelters, and taught the "cycle of violence." And I know the treatment for violence in the penitentiaries includes twelve-step programs, aversion therapy.

And in my working life, I've been forced to say, "the individual can change," "walk away from him," "break the cycle," "find a higher power." Take the individual to the universal. Bullshit.

None of that works for La Loche. None of that works anywhere. We need structural change.

Historians claim all true change is the result of *violent* revolution. They forget fire, agriculture, language, the wheel, which also r/evolves.

And now poets, the visionaries, truth-sayers, friends of the healer: what is our vision? Can we see beyond our own dung heap?

As poets, as thinking people, we have to search for something as basic, as unimagined, as quietly elegant as the wheel. A world where structural inequalities do not pit man against woman, race against race. A world where power is something offered to your community, not held over it as a fist.

Where healing is more important than achieving. Where healing *is* achieving.

Where "not feeling" is a sickness, not a desirable state, or a factor of survival.

Where the absence of love is not possible. Because then violence is not possible.

And there has to be a way to shape the path to that place through our words. Women have to lead the way. Women and "emotional men." Human beings.

I'm not talking about chipping away at racism, sexism, class inequalities. I don't mean we need more navel-gazing or earnest exposés.

The word "revolution" has been tarnished with overtones of violence, but it *is* revolution we need.

Let's construct a vision and live in it.

I want my children to live there.

I want to live there, too.

looking for meaning

1. She never did learn how to sing
not like those birds out there
the peregrine falcon
eating the robin
the seagull snatching the garbage
raven with entrails
hawk with infant rabbit

Or growl like the dog lunging at the wooden slats
as she walks by
the lion pissing from the platform in the pitiful concrete cage

She will run
like the deer before the hunter's spotlights
like the fox just ahead of the dogs and the deadly hooves
Every time she looks for meaning
for a message in the guts of the dead
and finds none

2. Wait. Here is a short life
here is a fish which ate a fish which ate a minnow
here is a crayfish still alive on the lake bottom
where she believed they had all washed ashore
grey and brittle

The salamander sliding into the dog dish
the frog escaping the child's netted hands
these earth lives she understands
their lowly expectation to survive
their many eyes a lesson in quickness
and the violent but true end to all things

such a beauty this
this meaninglessness.

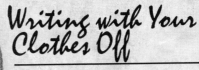

Writing with Your Clothes Off

SANDRA NICHOLLS

Sandra Nicholls has written everything from award-winning poetry to speeches for Federal Government Cabinet ministers to lyrics for songs performed and recorded by the jazz quartet Chelsea Bridge. In 1987 she won the *Food For Thought* Award from the Canadian Authors Association. Her first book, *The Untidy Bride* (Quarry Press), was short-listed for the 1991 Pat Lowther Award. In 1994, she won third prize in the international Stephen Leacock Poetry Competition. Her poems and short stories have appeared in literary magazines across Canada, including *Queen's Quarterly*, *The Antigonish Review*, and *Room of One's Own* and in anthologies including *Capital Poets*, *Open Set*, and *Vintage 93*. She has taught English literature and creative writing at both high school and university levels. Her second poetry collection, *Woman of Sticks, Woman of Stones* (Quarry Press), won the Archibald Lampman Award for Poetry in 1997.

Writing with Your Clothes Off

❦ ❧

Several years ago I attended a workshop on short story writing. Dutifully we submitted our stories, worked at and pored over in the small hours of the night in our close, hot, cramped dormitory rooms. Labored over, revised, polished, discussed, reworked . . . we submitted our stories to our advisors. My advisor was a well-respected male writer who remained unimpressed as I turned in story after story. *Don't quite grab me*, he'd say. *Can't quite get into them*, he'd say. *Why don't you try writing with your clothes off*, he said one day, and we got into a big argument. *Go and write about something that makes you angry*, he said, *go and get angry, write it down*. Ever hoping I might learn something, and furious at this point anyway, I went back to my room and raged over my word processor.

I had been reading about medieval painters who tried everything to avoid painting their subject's feet, and who sometimes left the feet right out of their paintings. Why? A phrase came into my head: *Because she knew all about running, but she couldn't move*. That phrase turned into a story. I hacked it out overnight and brought it to my advisor the next morning. He took it away and promised comments by the afternoon. When I met with him that same day, he handed the story back, unmarked, and said, *well, this is good, but it's a story about incest. That's what all you feminists write about these days, isn't it?* And with that, I was dismissed.

I got a similar response trying to get it published. Most editors agreed it was well written, evocative, and effective. But gee, there's that subject matter again. Sorry. Finally I got it published in a literary magazine from British Columbia — a feminist literary magazine — a magazine whose work I greatly respected, but all the same, a ghetto for women's writing.

For the first time in my writing life, I felt the frustration and humiliation of Shakespeare's sister, as Virginia Woolf described her — denied an outlet because I was a woman. "'Caught and tangled,' 'denied,' suffocated, self-buried, or not yet born," as Woolf put it, because I had chosen a "woman's" subject.[1] Yet pick up any five copies of current literary periodicals and review the subject matter of much of the poetry and short story material therein — men coping with divorce, men mooning over women (seemingly a tireless theme), men trying to cope with raising their children. All valid themes. But are they any more valid than incest?

What about stories written by *women* trying to cope with their families? With domestic life? Editors have pooh-poohed these themes for years. Except if men write about them, in which case they are courageous and ambitious. As Margaret Atwood said once, to the best of my recollection: "If a woman writes about doing the dishes, it's banal; if a man writes about doing the dishes, it is revolutionary."

The seeds of my own feminism were undergoing some rapid fertilization. I remembered what Theodore Roethke said when he reviewed the work of his friend Louise Bogan. He started out to point a finger at the typical criticisms women poets face, but then somehow he got carried away.

> Two of the [most frequent] charges . . . are lack of range — in subject matter, in emotional tone — and lack of a sense of humor. And one could, in individual instances among writers of real talent, add other aesthetic and moral shortcomings: the spinning out; the embroidering of trivial themes; a concern with the mere surfaces of life — that special province of the feminine talent in prose — hiding from the real agonies of the spirit; refusing to face up to what existence is; lyric or religious posturing; running between the boudoir and the altar; stamping a tiny foot against God or lapsing into a sentientiousness that implies the author has reinvented integrity; carrying on excessively about Fate, about time; lamenting the lot of the woman; caterwauling; writing the same poem about fifty times, and so on . . .[2]

Sandra Gilbert and Susan Gubar responded best to this critical attitude: "Shaking a Promethean male fist against God is one perfectly reasonable aesthetic strategy, apparently, but stamping a tiny feminine foot is quite another."[3] In other words, men can write about God, fate, time, and integrity, but women can't. But if I wanted to write about incest, that wouldn't do either. So neither "men's" nor "women's" subject matter was appropriate?

When *A Room of One's Own* was originally conceived, it formed part of two papers Virginia Woolf delivered to Cambridge students in 1928, the year after she published *To the Lighthouse*. In *Room,* she shares the ideas which led her to conclude that if a woman is to be able to write, she must have "money and a room of her own."

They seem like simple conditions, although they are still too rare. Knowing this may point to answers to questions like, why are women so absent from books on literature or history; why is so little written about the history of women? Not that long ago, the *Norton Anthology of English Literature* contained only two works by women, two short poems by Lady Montague. And yet this book was considered part of the canon of literature. Part of an immutable history of the world. Half of whose inhabitants were almost invisible.

Virginia Woolf pointed out that it had been relatively easy for her to come to writing, since the way had been paved by female writers such as Aphra Behn, Jane Austen, and George Eliot. Yet current studies of Woolf suggest it may have been her struggle to reconcile being a woman with being a writer, the frustrations of either/or, that led her to fill her pockets with stones and drown herself in the River Ouse in 1947.

For in her subject matter, Virginia Woolf experimented with form. She tried to capture the moment of experience, a character's individual perceptions and impressions, as received in the mind. She discarded traditional elements of plot and character and journeyed into the minds of her characters. She also sought a feminine form of language, a new way of expressing reality.

Sounds ambitious to me. Yet reading an essay on Woolf included in a 1969 *Pelican Guide to English Literature,* I was distressed to find the word "limitations" crop up about five times in reference to her scope, ability, and purpose. *A Room of One's Own* is described as interesting and occasionally amusing. She is slapped on the wrist for being strident, "prejudiced against the tyranny of the male intellect," and incapable of "describing the subtleties and complications of normal, mature living."[4]

In *To the Lighthouse* she tries to describe the role of the artist in bringing together two sides of the self, two ways of seeing the world: the factual, linear, masculine view of Mr. Ramsay, and the intuitive, non-linear, feminine view of Mrs. Ramsay. But Penguin's agitated male critic points out that: "It is a weakness of Virginia Woolf's novels that her models of mature, feminine wisdom are essentially adolescent — Mrs. Ramsay has an untrained mind."[5] So much for balance. No wonder Woolf's creation, the hypothetical Judith Shakespeare, denied access to learning, to an income of her own, to a room of her own, ends up dead at the crossroads of the Elephant and Castle, "tortured and pulled asunder by her own contrary instincts."[6] Yet despite the bitter pill Woolf is asking us to swallow, she seldom sounds angry. In fact, she is almost light-hearted, even as she replies to the bishop who declared that it is "impossible for any woman, past, present, or to come, to have the genius of Shakespeare."[7] She commends Jane Austen for writing "without hate, without bitterness, without fear, without protest, without preaching."[8] She pities the seventeenth-century poet Lady Winchelsea because her mind was "forced to anger and bitter."[9]

But it is difficult *not* to get angry as Woolf describes the conditions necessary for creativity and then goes on to point out how often women have been denied them. She enrages, she provokes, and thinly she veils her own anger.

For Virginia Woolf understood too well the double standard that erupts when it comes to women's writing. In 1929 she wrote:

> When a woman comes to write a novel, she will find that she is perpetually wishing to alter the established values — to make serious what appears insignificant to a man, and trivial what to him is important. And for that, of course, she will be criticized; for the critic of the opposite sex will be genuinely puzzled and surprised by an attempt to alter the current scale of values, and will see in it not merely a difference of view, but a view that is weak, or trivial, or sentimental because it differs from his own.[10]

Genuinely puzzled. Things have changed. Women's anger has produced a flood of literature. Women's courses are being introduced. Women are beginning to be able to find mirrors of their own experience in the works they study at school, mirrors which lend authenticity and resonance to their concerns and ideas.

No longer do we have to accept statements such as the one made by the critic R.P. Blackmuir, who opined that Emily Dickinson was "neither a professional poet nor an amateur; she was a private poet who wrote indefatigably, as some women cook or knit. Her gift for words and the cultural predicament of her time drove her to poetry instead of antimacassars."[11] As if Shakespeare wrote as some men hunted or went bowling, as if his gift for words drove him to poetry instead of duck decoys.

So it came as a surprise that I reacted as I did when the publishers of my first book of poetry, *The Untidy Bride,* sent me the copy for the back cover. I was described as writing in a distinctly *feminist* voice. Well, yes, I considered my*self* a feminist, but I found myself struggling with all kinds of questions. Would this qualifier limit my audience? Would it conscript my book to women's bookstores? Was it really a feminist voice? Was there a clearly understood definition of what feminist stood for? Did my book fit into that category? In my classroom where I taught literature the students had no doubt I was a feminist. Was I afraid to label myself one?

I found myself fighting a label. I panicked at the thought of being so *defined.* It was as if I had to pin down the concerns expressed between the covers of my book. Poems about my father's death. How were these feminist? Would the feelings have been different if I'd not considered myself a feminist? Poems about menstruation, mothers, marriages. These? How? What did it mean? Did I think the way I did because I was a feminist or because I was, well, *me?*

Woolf's frustration with either/or drove her to suicide. Our obsession with it continues to fill our world with violent separations. We live in a world where women are raped in the name of ethnic cleansing, where people and territory are carved out and subdivided, walled in and walled out. You are a Muslim, a Serb, a Hindu, Arab, Jew. I was a feminist, or I was not. I saw that I was falling into the very trap I was trying to avoid, subscribing to either/or thinking while trying to shake it off. But the questions wouldn't stop: who would I shut out by labelling myself; who would I fail to reach?

Good friends were appalled by my stance. They reminded me about the sisters who had gone before, the women who had fought for access to literacy and the printed word, those without whom I would have had no book to argue about, those I had been talking about all year to my students. Did I want to identify myself with an entire generation of young women who are convinced they have won everything they have on their own and who are loathe to call themselves feminists?

I struggled to define my own uneasiness. I wrote back to the publishers requesting them to simply say, "written in a distinctive voice." Somehow my poems had been "caught and tangled" in an entire social, cultural, and economic movement. It was assumed I shared a set of values and beliefs, when I wondered if we'd even found such unanimity.

In her introduction to *The Second Sex*, Simone de Beauvoir said:

> In the midst of an abstract discussion it is vexing to hear a man say: "You think thus and so because you are a woman," but I know that my only defence is to reply, "I think thus and so because it is true," thereby removing my subjective self from the argument. It would be out of the question to reply: "And you think the contrary because you are a man," for it is understood that the fact of being a man is no peculiarity.[12]

I hoped what I had to say was true, at least to my own experience. Yet somehow, by focusing on the feminist voice, it seemed as if the *feminism* was more important than the *voice* itself, as if the *I* had been somehow eclipsed. Men's voices were not defined as part of a larger movement. They were simply allowed to exist, in all their diverse and idiosyncratic noise. That was the freedom I wanted. To think thus and so because it was true. To say it to anyone, not just feminists.

Perhaps I must learn to embrace the contradictions within my own definition, so that I do not contribute to the same fanaticism which refuses to allow differences to exist. Perhaps, as a friend said, I need a new definition of feminism. Or perhaps I just need to define it for myself, to "re-vision" it in my own terms. A quest every woman has to undertake for herself. As Adrienne Rich put it:

> To question everything. To remember what has been forbidden even to mention. To come together telling our stories, to look afresh at, and then to describe for ourselves, the frescoes of the Ice Age, the nudes of "High Art," the Minoan seals and figurines, the moon-landscape embossed with the booted print of a male boot, the microscopic virus, the scarred and tortured body of the planet Earth.[13]

To look afresh at, and then to describe for ourselves. As I needed to do. As we all need to do, with eloquence, urgency, and intelligence.

1. Mary Eagleton, Ed., *Feminist Literary Theory: A Reader* (Oxford: Basil Blackwood, 1990), p. 107.

2. Eagleton, p. 107.

3. Eagleton, P. 108.

4. Boris Ford, ed., *The Pelican Guide to English Literature* (Aylebury: Penguin, 1969), pp. 265-67.

5. Ford, pp. 265-67.

6. Virginia Woolf, *A Room of One's Own* (London: Grafton Books, 1989), p. 48.

7. Woolf, p. 45.

8. Woolf, p. 65.

9. Woolf, p. 58.

10. Woolf, p. 58.

11. Eagleton, p. 108.

12. Simone be Beauvoir, *The Second Sex* (New York: Vintage, 1989), p. xxi.

13. Adrienne Rich, *On Lies, Secrets, and Silence* (New York: Norton, 1979), p. 13.

The Woman in the Wall

From the absence of visions
of voices or signs, I turn
my face to the wall,
press my ear to the floral paper.
The woman must be inside
her teeth splintered with wood
her nails crusted with white dust
from the struggle to get out.
I have created her
from the scraping inside me
I refuse to hear
in the deep pit of the afternoon
or long into the night,
the body is a clever old trickster
to locate itself elsewhere:
in the groove of an old record
or under the carpets,
the body is also terrified,
throwing its voice
from inside the wall, or calling
on the phone, disguised
as your mother, you're always blind
to its coming, until one day
you stop listening,
it's this or it's that or it's anything
but me, the moon, the weather,
the time of year,
the walls begin to peel away like skin:
there is no one inside.

this black ball we carry around inside us

DI BRANDT

Di Brandt grew up in a Mennonite community in southern Manitoba. Her first book of poetry, *questions I asked my mother* (Turnstone), received the Gerald Lampert Memorial Award and was nominated for both the Governor General's Award and the Dillon Commonwealth Prize. She won the Canadian Authors Award for 1995 as well as the National Mag Award for Poetry. Her second collection, *Agnes in the Sky* (Turnstone), won the McNally Robinson Award for Manitoba Book of the Year. Her third collection was *mother, not mother* (Mercury); her fourth collection, *Jerusalem, beloved* (Turnstone) was nominated for the Governor General's Award. She is also the author of a critical study of maternal narrative in Canadian literature, *Wild Mother Dancing* (University of Manitoba Press), as well as *Dancing Naked: Strategies for Writing across Centuries* (Mercury). Di Brandt teaches creative writing and English at the University of Winnipeg and has served as Writer-in-Residence at the University of Alberta in Edmonton.

this black ball we carry around inside us

❧ ❧

I grew up in a pacifist culture. my Mennonite ancestors were violently dispossessed of their homes & turned into more or less permanent refugees in Europe, for several centuries, for refusing to participate in war, for refusing to baptise their children as infants (insisting upon the innocence of children), and for speaking out against the structural hierarchy of the Catholic church (insisting on the right of conscience for each person individually & for the group as a democracy). i grew up with stories of my dad & his friends heroically refusing the draft during the second world war, & having to spend several years in CO camp [for conscientious objectors] &/or prison as a result. i also grew up with a daily rhetoric of non-violence, turning the other cheek, understanding, forgiveness & reconciliation instead of revenge. there were never any loud words spoken in my house, & we were not allowed to express anger, or use words that implied violence of any kind.

that's the official story. the unofficial story is that the children in my community were ritually beaten by their fathers at an early age, usually under a year old, in front of other family members, and usually against their mother's wishes, to instill obedience & the fear of the Lord in them. adolescents were not allowed to express their individuality, & women were not allowed to contradict their husbands at home or elsewhere, or to speak in public. when i started writing poetry & performing it, i hallucinated a lot. i had visions of the floor caving in, the room spinning, the ocean roaring in my head, & everything going black. i also had a fantasy that lasted for several years, that someone, a committee of Mennonite men, would come to my house & shoot me for daring to break the taboos of the culture. an alternate recurring fantasy was suicide.

in june 1991, after five years of therapy & three books of poetry & two years of yoga practice, i had a stunning flashback to a trauma that occurred when i was perhaps five weeks old. my uncle Peter, my dad's brother, was raping me, orally, with a huge, gigantic penis, almost as big as my head. after that, he tried to strangle me with his hands around my neck. i've been reliving the horror of this memory now for several years. i have spent hundreds of dollars learning to be angry, angry as hell, to make fists & to fight back, not with guns & knives & ropes, which are recurring images in my recent poems. but with personal strength & clarity of vision. & most of all, with words, which are coming in handy at last.

shortly after i had the memory, i spent several weeks in Jerusalem, on a Canada Council grant, visiting an old friend & trying to write poetry. the atmosphere of violence in Israel & occupied Palestine was shocking, stunning, & all-pervasive. it felt exactly like the violence in my memory, & i started remembering, if that's the word, the violent perse-cution that happened to Mennonites during the Reformation purges in Europe, & felt, very tangibly, in my bones, the way these historical events were connected to my family experience.

i was very impressed, in Jerusalem, with the cheerful, passionate, heroic acts of resistance i witnessed among the Palestinians, against the occupation of their country. i was also struck by the similarity between Israeli acts of brutality against Palestinians & what happened to Jews in the holocaust during the second world war. i looked at the people living in refugee camps in Gaza, & thought, they've been living like that for forty years, there are still people old enough to remember a time when things were different, when children didn't throw rocks at soldiers on the way to school & come home with broken faces and knees, when fathers didn't experience daily routines of humiliation & helplessness against military force. i thought, in another forty years, these people will start inflicting violence on each other, in their work & family rela-tionships, openly or covertly, if they're not doing it already, because they will have forgotten that this isn't a normal way to live, they won't remember how not to do it anymore.

& i thought i understood why people choose to make war on each other, why men beat their wives and children & rape them, why women are prevented from public speech & decision-making power. i thought i understood how public and personal violence are interconnected, & how the only way to stop it is for each person to withdraw into silence & self-reflection & grief & self-transformation, to come to terms with their own personal & cultural history of violence, & then to speak about it. that is the only way to stop the terrible cycle.

there are no words in me for Gaza, for what i saw
in Gaza, the eyes of the women lining up at the
hospital for milk, with their babies & small
children, their eyes looking at me, another North
American tourist with nothing to offer, except
terrible pity, & shame, shame at my innocence,
my stupid privilege, i never imagined such a place,
i could have been born here, & thought this is what
the world is like, these narrow streets filled with
flies & cowdung, shacks made of sheet metal &
bare wooden boards, the path to the beach littered
with barbed wire & abandoned jeeps, & grey sand,
how long does it take to forget, the soldiers at the
door, the women screaming, the broken china,
embroidered tablecloths flapping in the wind,
blood running from the father's mouth, how long
does it take to forget, the darkness in this woman's
eyes, the children hiding rocks in their hands on
the way to school, these two will not come home
tonight, their shins broken by soldiers in the street,
these eyes, the long long sorrow in them, these
women's eyes, looking at me

how long does it take to forget a murder in your
house, behind a closed door, without a sound, no
words said, the hanging in a field your great
grandmother watched as a little girl, her face pushed
against her father's sleeve, a heretic slow burning at
the end of August in the town square? how long
does the body remember the bullet, where it graced
the flesh, the cells burned, blue black, where it
entered skin, nerve endings charred, trembling?
how long does it take to forget a gas chamber filled
with naked, terrified, bearded men, the roomful
of women, the accused, sentenced to burning, a
soldier's rifle under the chin, cocked, the soldier's
hand, shaking, full of hatred, shame, rage?

this black ball we carry around inside us, this
darkness, this red flaming sea, how it comes back
to us, this violence, to haunt us, a ghost, the devil, the
enemy, how it yearns, like tree roots, to take hold, to
flower in us, like branches & leaves:

the body's humiliation, trembling, how it stays in
the air, long after the body is gone, dismembered, the
spirit seeking revenge – or is it comforting it wants,
remembering, shaking, grieving, so we will not do it
again, to someone else, the way it was done to us, so
that the flowering can be trembling, beautiful, wise,
as newborn children are, instead of wrath?

Counting to Ten

MAJA BANNERMAN

Maja Bannerman writes poems, songs, and performance pieces. Raised in Ottawa and Sault Ste. Marie, she moved first to Toronto, then Seattle, and now lives in rural Ontario, where she pursues a singing and performing career. She has performed across Canada in galleries, libraries, and classrooms with musician David Prentice. Her one-woman show of monologues and songs, *First and Third Person*, was produced at Theatre Passe Muraille in Toronto. Her publications include *Frontispiece* with Philip Adams, *Songs Poems Performance Pieces* (Blewointmentpress), and the tapes *Future Perfect* (Onari), *Via Satellite* (White Jasmin), *Make a Wish* (White Jasmin), and *The Golden Veil* (White Jasmin). Her work has been anthologized in *Into the Night* and *Poets in the Classroom*. She is a continuing contributor to the literary periodical *paperplates*.

Counting to Ten

❧ ❦

As writers, we are able to help define struggles and search for solutions with our words, and perhaps we are therefore suited to tackling difficult and complex issues. Here, we are asked to consider two matters: the relationship between domestic and international violence, and the possibility for reconciliation. In my comments I'll refer to my work with the Central America Project Office of Peace Brigades International and to my experience of being a Quaker (member of the Religious Society of Friends) in the context of my own desire to look at, not violence *around* me, but violence *within myself.*

Domestic and international, public violence seem to me to be similar in type rather than in method. Although in both cases the violence can be verbal or physical, the more sophisticated mechanisms are found on the international scale: tools and training for torture and killing as well as access to disinformation services, including television, radio, and print media. My father used to say to me, when I asked "why?" about something, to ask instead, "who is making the money?" The desire for power, which is often related to economics, is the common element in both the private and social worlds of violence.

In the domestic arena, disinformation is called emotional blackmail and can be inflicted with words and/or silences. Here violent physical actions and reactions are less controlled because there is no "official" orchestrator standing outside the violence, determining its beginning and ending. Feeling ineffectual in other aspects of life, the aggressor chooses violence, gaining thereby a sense of power. Violence becomes an easy way to avoid dealing with other areas of one's life.

The National Clearing House on Family Violence has stated: "The use of corporal punishment in the home, as a form of discipline, legitimizes violence and gives young people the mistaken message that force is an indication of love." Children learn that adults often express their feeling of frustration in an abusive or violent manner. Luckily children can also learn that there are other ways to deal with their aggression.

I like to think our society has become more aware of alternatives to violence for dealing with conflict. But I realize that, although there has been an increase in interest in workshops about civilian-based defence and other methods of aggressive nonviolent resistance among a small group, it has not had an effect on the mainstream of society.

One of the strong, positive features of nonviolent action is that it doesn't require material resources and can consequently be used by those without financial advantage. By learning how to disarm people or how to disengage from conflict without violence, one can open up a space for mediation and conciliation.

I'd like to include a couple of examples of how civilian-based defence and other techniques have been used for protection or to disarm someone in potentially violent situations in the public arena.

> During one of the many 19th-century riots in Paris, a commander of an army detachment received orders to clear a city square by firing at the people. He commanded his soldiers to take up firing positions, their rifles levelled at the crowd, and as the people grew silent, the commander shouted that he had received orders to shoot at the rabble. But as he saw that there were a great number of respectable citizens there, he requested that they leave first. In a few minutes the square was cleared without the use of guns.[1]

Another useful method is the confusion technique. Confronted with a potentially violent situation one offers a response that is confusing and creates a space either for verbal communication to take place or for withdrawal from the situation. For instance, someone bumps into you very aggressively and your normal response may be to apologize and say you're sorry. Instead you tell the person the incorrect time, removing the aggressive contact completely from the situation and, by creating confusion, provide an opportunity to disengage. It's true these are methods of avoidance and not negotiation. They do not solve conflicts but definitely diffuse the aggressive energy that is ignited in such situations.

One of the services offered by Peace Brigades International is an accompaniment/escort service for Central Americans threatened by violence. By having a third party, an international observer, present, death squads and paramilitary groups are deterred from committing acts of violence. The volunteers also use cameras to record any threatening person or situation. The cameras are considered important tools, or weapons, as some volunteers call them.

During the invasion of Czechoslovakia, the citizens changed street signs around, so that invaders could not easily find their way. This kind of action would be considered a technique of civilian-based defence. Such actions give people a sense of empowerment and control.

One of my own concerns is how to adapt these methods to the personal situation — how to deal with my own capacity for, and expression of, violence. I find it helpful to define violence as an *act* and *not* an emotion, and to try to determine what situations make me feel trapped in violent expression. Researching this, I read recently:

> It is true that violent action can have an energizing effect; however, this is achieved not by violence as such, but by the taking of positive action for a definite goal. There is no reason why vigorous nonviolent action should not be just as liberating, through giving one a sense of identity, power, and achievement.[2]

This statement gives me hope because I know it is the sudden rush of adrenalin in violent situations that can trigger violent action, and if I can learn techniques that incorporate my physical response, it will enable me to release that energy without the devastating effects of violent expression. I also know that if I hadn't been writing since I was little, I'd be in an even less advantageous position to learn new ways of behaving. Writing has always been a therapeutic act: an uncovering, discovering, and recovering, though the pencil was pressed so fiercely on the page, the lead broke again and again. Reading about nonviolent methods and hearing about others' experiences, I realize there *are* alternatives and I am not thrashing about in a vacuum. This is liberating. There are places to hold on. I've titled this essay "Counting to Ten"; that's not always easy to do.

---

1. Paul Watzlawick, John Weakland, Richard Fisch, *Change — Principles of Problem Formation and Problem Resolution* (New York: Norton, 1974), p. 81.
2. Phillips D. Moulton, Pendle Hill Pamphlet # 178 (Pendle Hill, 1971).

Family Reunion

There's one funny photograph:
all the kids got into the
whirlpool tub, raised glasses to the New Year,
they were laughing and cheering.

Later the same night
I was gathering all the kitchen knives
and hiding them under the red rec-room carpet.

My mother crouched on the floor
hands over her head
as my father and brother
screamed and screamed at her.

And then I screamed too.
My mother's whimpering
the wall of sound
our voices bounced around
Wagnerian.

Frantic, I wanted to call for help,
appeal to my other brothers for rescue.
I counted to ten over and over and over again
then
just wanted to get the hell out.
I stepped outside into the Arctic cold
and howling at the moon
I saw my world freezing over.

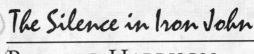

The Silence in Iron John
RICHARD HARRISON

Richard Harrison is the author of *Fathers Never Leave You* (Mosaic Press), *Recovering the Naked Man* (Wolsak & Wynn), *Hero of the Play* (Wolsak & Wynn), which was launched at the Hockey Hall of Fame, and *Big Breath of a Wish* (Wolsak & Wynn). His awards include the Harbourfront and the Milton Acorn Prize. He is a frequent guest speaker and reader of his poems in schools, university classes, and public venues; he has served as the Canadian Writer-in-Residence at the University of Calgary in the Markin-Flanagan Distinguished Writers Program. His work has been anthologized in *A Discord of Flags, Thru the Smoky End Boards, Canadian Poetry about Sports and Games,* and *Vintage 96.* Richard Harrison has has been featured on "Adrienne Clarkson Presents," and his inaugural reading in Calgary was held at the Saddledome.

The Silence in Iron John

❦

Lately men have thrown a lot of words at the problem of their silence. They have attempted to break their personal silence by writing about their previously unexpressed feelings. They have attempted to the stop silencing of others by beginning to call patriarchal oppression by name.

To stop silencing others means listening, listening hard and well. What is said is terrible to hear: *DON'T: A Woman's Word;* the indigenous peoples' history of North America after Columbus; the Clarence Thomas hearings. Our mothers and sisters have been raped and told the blame is theirs. Men who listen feel intense shame and guilt and anger.

But for men to stop silencing also means hearing that the pain of others is not like our own because it comes in part out of their oppression as a class. In a good-faith world, men's shame and guilt and anger would be channelled to self-inspection and political change. But, as many feminist authors are pointing out, there is a strong backlash, an attempt to silence again the newly speaking voices, re-marginalize the stories, treat the question as if it were only a matter of personal blame and ragingly refuse to take the guilt.

Supposedly against this backlash is the work of Robert Bly, Sam Keene, and others in the "Men's Movement." These works attempt to release (supposedly) previously unexpressed feelings of abandonment, rage at women, and anger at the longed-for father in the group of men largely defined by the sale of hard-cover books: Bly's so called "soft men," educated, 30–40 year olds who have been — as all boys have been since the Industrial Revolution — separated from their fathers and the real goodness in and of the masculine. These works attempt to revive Good Male Power, call it the Wild Man, the King Within, the God Inside, and so on. They try to let these men reclaim their connections to other men, the Universal Masculine, and themselves through a combination of argument, a re-working of myth and fable, and the re-enactment of the rituals of passage by which other, healthier societies mark the distinction between big boys and true men. The corollary good, it is claimed, is that true men do not beat women, but protect them. They do not fear women, they encourage them. The Men's Movement, its writers claim, is Feminism's friend and complement.

However, in its way — a very real and I think dangerous way — this movement embraces a kind of silence that, in the long run if not now, makes it part of the opposition to feminism. In "Why Iron John Is No Gift to Women" (*New York Times Book Review,* 23 February 1992), Jill Johnston argues that the men's movement has adopted the language, approach, and (my word) tactics of the feminist movement to achieve its ends without acknowledging that the feminist movement's aim is to liberate women as a class. For example, the re-presentation of the Goddess is a means of class liberation. It provides members of an oppressed class with previously denied models of personal power. Men as a class are already empowered, so the current re-presentation of male God-figures and heroes by Bly and others validates the already present principle of dominance. For those in the men's movement, men have lost something to feminism that needs to be taken back from women. By taking on the search for myths and mythic figures, the men's movement has modelled itself on those conceptual aspects of the feminist movement that allow it to present men as being a group in need of power. But it also enforces the two silences of patriarchy that it claims to break. Any dissent within the movement is explained in terms of the individual's failure to have re-empowered himself along the mythically described lines. And, since the myths and stories the men's movement chooses are divided along strict gender lines, women's stories are once again peripheral, part of women's empowerment, not men's.

Iron John, the Wild Man, The King, and so on are all fillers for the dominant figure in men's movement thinking: the absent male. But both the absent figure (mentor, father) and the focal figure (King, Iron John) are mythic. They represent the mysterious Man who is sometimes seen in an individual man, and whom all men strive to be. What he is lies within all men. What he is not is the body of the present man. He is not the man of history. Rather, he is a spirit, an energy who can be discovered through the body, its humiliation, its wounding, perhaps its joy. But he is not the body.

One of feminism's most important contributions is the validation of the body, making the body's story more important than the myth, making the words on the page the writing of the body. Men's movement work is doing exactly the opposite, using the body to bring about the return of the Real Figure who lies below the surface, and who must be freed from it by the actions of men.

I'll speak in the story's own terms: freeing Iron John from the bottom of a lake where he lies confined by water (like a fetus?) leads a young prince to his own emancipation from his mother and father (the entanglement with the mother is the more difficult to break). A frightening figure to the civilized world with his body covered in rust-coloured hair, Iron John guides the boy through a series of bodily trials which ultimately transform him into a self-sufficient (warrior) man. There are two things I want to note:

1. The role of women in the story. Women in *Iron John* are either, according to Johnston, psychological impediments (mother) or personal rewards (the Princess). I would add two other roles. Women are also either political opponents (witches) whose power must be taken after battle, or they are the ones who recognize and validate male power. Taken together these four exhaust the possibilities for women. The distinction between heroic and villainous acquisitions of woman-as-reward is that the hero is the one the woman is represented as going to willingly. The real man has power the woman recognizes and is thankful for.

2. The role of the voice of women in the book. *Iron John,* and I see this in other texts too, uses deference to feminism to silence women. Often Bly will describe a psychological or social process in young men on their way to adulthood. He does not deny that there may be a similar process in women, but he does not discuss it. Instead he says, "a woman can speak on this better than I," before moving on with the boy-man's story. No doubt a woman can speak better than Bly about "this." But the point is that, with the exception of the four roles described above, the making of a man is man's work. It is not

society's work. Bly speaks admiringly of what he describes as secret, sacred rituals in which men and boys withdraw from their community to do the work of changing boys to men. In both the argument of Bly's book, and the folk-tale on which it is based, women are not speaking subjects with a weight and wisdom equal to that of the male mother-figure and mentor represented by Iron John himself. They are necessary steps in the physical and emotional process of the making of a man.

Equally, the body of the boy is reduced to a locus of necessary steps in the revelation of the Man within. There is no place, and no language for a place, for the particularity of memory, of pleasure, of pain, of fear of death, of digestion and farting, of remembering birth, of re-inventing birth and its attachment to the blood of the mother's body, or of remembering the father in any other aspect than anger and fear which eventually gives way to awe. There is no change in the way of speaking, and no challenge to the way of telling the tale. The objections within the story, that is, the body of the hearer, are silenced, and no other way of telling is allowed.

And this exclusivity, which redraws the map of the Universal Man on each man, is only re-enforced by the structure of the men's movement group, modelled on what I believe is the necessary (for the moment) exclusivity of groups of women, and of others who are gathering their political strength by mutual reliance. Men's groups are playing out the initial concept of each man as an example of the Universal Man who needs others only as parts of his own creation, a creation which supersedes any alternative concept of man. Nor does *Iron John* challenge the social inequalities it claims to redress. While posturing inclusion, it ushers woman's voice outside the sacred circle in which it works. *Iron John* is an utterance which affirms the very silences it claims to break.

Rhéaume

Here is the desire of Manon Rhéaume: to stop the
puck. Come down from the stands, strap on the big
pads, painted mask, disappear into *goalie* the way
a man can be a man and not a man inside the
armour. To forget in the motion of the save that we
do not forget she is always a woman and sex is
everything: if she wasn't pretty she'd never hear her
looks got her on the NHL team in Tampa Bay
where the ushers are women hired from a bar
called *Hooters,* and David Letterman wouldn't have
her on *Late Night* prodding her again and again, *Say
Ocke-ee;* if Brett Hull was ugly as a wet owl and
scored 86 goals a season, still there'd be kids with
his poster on their bedroom doors. To be a woman
and have it be her play that counts. To stop the
puck where the best are men, for men to be better
than they are. On your wall is a collage of women
with their arms raised, they are dancing, they are
lifting weights, they are marching against apartheid.
One is a goddess with snakes in her hands;
Catwoman reaches for Gotham, Boadicea shakes a
spear in the face of Rome, two nuns run splashing
into the laughing waves: here, I give you Rhéaume
and a glove save, the puck heading for the top
corner. Stopped.

The Mis/Shape of the Evidence

NADINE MCINNIS

Nadine McInnis is the author of three books of poetry, *Shaking the Dreamland Tree* (Coteau Books), *The Litmus Body* (Quarry Press), which won the 1993 Ottawa-Carleton Book Award and was short-listed for the Pat Lowther Award, and *Hand to Hand* (Polestar), as well as one book of criticism, *Poetics of Desire: Nadine McInnis on Dorothy Livesay* (Turnstone). She has also been awarded First Prize in the 1992 National Poetry Contest of the League of Canadian Poets and the Nepean Library Short Story Contest in 1993. She is a past prize-winner of the CBC Literary Competition. Her work has been anthologized in *Up and Doing: Canadian Women and Peace*, *Kitchen Talk*, and *New Women Writers*. More recently, she has been writing short fiction, with stories appearing in *The Malahat Review*, *Grain*, *Quarry*, and *Canadian Fiction Magazine*.

The Mis/Shape of the Evidence

※ ❦

We can agree on what we see when faced with violence in its visceral form. Wars, torture, random acts that spill blood. All of this is the raw material of art, but the really *necessary* work of writers, because no-one else can do it, is to expose what we can't yet agree that we see. A writer makes visible what was dangerously invisible. This is not as easy as it sounds. I want to talk about some of the struggles I've had with the violent content in my own writing and the resistance I've faced.

I have not led a violent life. I'm one of the lucky women who reached adulthood without being sexually assaulted, beaten, or abused. But I was an early witness to self-destructiveness, alcoholism, and suicide attempts hidden beneath the surface of the middle-class family I came from. Moving to a reserve in northern Saskatchewan when I was twenty-three confirmed what I had always sensed. Here was a peaceful community, people whose quiet lives were intermittently shattered by tragedies. It felt familiar to me. It was largely a difference in degree. What seemed invisible in my family: the alcoholism, the self-destructiveness which is a form of violence, the despair, were kept invisible by the blessing of being one of many, by being middle-class and white, by fitting in. But it wouldn't take much to disrupt all that uneasy order. Writing about it, making it visible, is a tremendous threat. My own writing is denied by my parents. They will not acknowledge what I've written. Not a word. I've explored some of the dark areas not just of my own life, but of theirs, and perhaps they think I will stop if I don't get any attention. Like a bad child, perhaps I will grow out of it.

This is a personal difficulty many of us share. Recently, though, my vision as a writer has been used to undermine my credibility in a legal context, and it is this kind of resistance that I want to talk about because it is so hard to believe such a thing can happen in Canada. But it can; it's happening to me right now.

It began when I experienced psychic violence and sexual aggression directed at me by a psychiatrist I saw for several years. Another invisible kind of violence. What he did and how it affected me is another long, long story. I'll skip, instead, to his line of defence after I filed a complaint with the Ontario College of Physicians and Surgeons. Given prominence in his written defence was a bad review of my first book, which he used to try to prove that my vision of men and the world is deluded. He called the review "an accurate assessment of [my] psychodynamics," trying to pawn it off as an expert opinion. The basic gist of both the review and his use of it was that the world is not the way I see it. I'm just one of those man-hating feminists who perceives violation everywhere, even where it doesn't exist. My second book, *The Litmus Body,* was written during the time when I was experiencing the doctor's aggression, and the frightening undercurrent of everything from motherly love to writing itself is even more heightened in the poems. So how can anybody believe what I say?

This may seem like a bizarre and isolated situation, but it opened my eyes. Every time someone picks up a pen, the stakes are very high, whether they are writing a review, a defence, or a poem. My situation is in essence no different from that of the political writer anywhere in the world who is punished for writing a version of reality that doesn't conform to propaganda. It's a matter of basic human rights, this right to express oneself without losing the respect and protection of the law. But the law defines the perimeters of socially accepted behavior, whereas writers have always been there on the margins saying: "No, it's not like that. That's not how humans are. They are not what the law prescribes."

Maybe only the artist can offer a link between seeing and healing. Certainly not the institutions established to manage violence and the damage it leaves behind. Our institutions will never see and heal; they can only react to behaviors. This artistic vision of violence can be so threatening to a system which insists on the invisibility of the links between daily life and violence that the vision must be rejected. Of course, there will always be the reviewer who doesn't want to hear, the objections from the audience. This is part of a healthy dialogue, no matter how slanted some reviews and reactions may be. But when someone's opinions about a writer's work are used to undermine that writer's credibility in a court, it becomes obvious that it is *too* threatening: not only must the vision be rejected, the person who puts it forward must be punished and marginalized.

What is strange is that medicine and law both use the power of storytelling for their own ends. What happens in any court of law is storytelling, the presentation of adversarial versions to produce what is accepted as the best and most balanced version of reality. The legal profession's attention to language in this process is admirable. Medicine, particularly psychotherapy, relies on storytelling to reveal and re-interpret the past, and therefore alter patterns that affect the future. But these two institutions are not really about seeing in new ways. Precedents, which govern the interpretation of the law, are all about authority. Psychiatry is founded on theories of normal human development that distort the reality of at least fifty per cent of the human race. But how can we expect to find challenges coming from those who have always been most rewarded by things exactly how they are? It falls to us, to those watching from the edges, to challenge and reveal, to disorient those who think they lead lives of perfect balance.

Postscript

This story does exist in the linear world, and as it touches on so many writers' concerns, it deserves to be brought up to date. When I presented the above text at the 1992 Annual General Meeting of the League of Canadian Poets, I had only encountered the preliminary challenges to my voice as a writer. Ahead of me still were all the other challenges to my voice through my journals, medical records, testimony, and the explosive power of the media. Although these other trials were not specific to me as a writer, they did touch on many of our cultural concerns as writers: concerns of voice, text, and authority.

Hearings such as the College of Physicians and Surgeons' are quasi-legal, following the rules of evidence established in civil court, but the standard applied to a finding of guilt is much more rigorous, closer to that of criminal proceedings. One must be found guilty beyond a reasonable doubt. The civil standard for evidence, however, casts a much wider net than that allowed by a criminal proceeding. Into that net could fall my poems, my reviews, and my personal journals — any personal information or documents that might privilege the doctor's diagnosis of the mental "problem" that would result in me making such charges against him. My doctor introduced the original book review as part of his own written defence to sway the initial committee who would decide if he must face a formal hearing. Once it was determined that he would face a formal hearing, his lawyers went after my journals.

One of the strangest rules of evidence that was revealed during the process concerned my journal writing. The prosecutor told me she was not allowed to enter my hand-written journals as evidence, even though I had carefully documented the therapy week by week, but that the defence had the right to demand all the material I wrote while in therapy and could question me on intimate details even if they did not enter the journals as evidence. Surely, I thought, the absurdity of this must have been obvious. But no, the legal system, in all high seriousness, plays out our post-modern revolution, our post-modern anxieties. What is authority? What is voice? How can we trust or privilege any one voice, given how reality slips and slides, superimposing voice upon voice?

Certainly my doctor stepped over the line even in legal terms, but not until he had secured copies of his original medical records — without my authorization — that were in the possession of my subsequent doctor, and then altered them to reflect his version of my experiences on dates in question. He used my own journal entries to provide the structure to throw his own weird echoes against, date by date: I was borderline psychotic, I claimed to hear things that were never said, I was out of touch with reality. Thus my medical records now offered an alternate version, refuting my journal entries.

My second doctor has since been referred for a disciplinary hearing for releasing my records without my authorization. (Unknown to me at the time, he was also facing unrelated charges of sexual impropriety and professional misconduct during this same period; eventually, he was formally reprimanded.) Because the originals of these records have vanished with my first doctor when he fled to Argentina, the issue is not whether they were altered, but whether they were handled inappropriately. So all the motivation and significance have been stripped out of this story. It has become banal and bureaucratic. And six years later, I'm still waiting for my day to speak for myself, give my testimony in my own voice.

How did this story end? Well, it didn't; it escalated, and a process that started with a tentative letter, and swallowed my poems, reviews of my writing, my personal journals, medical records, bogus and true, and six years of my life and counting, was eventually swept into a media storm. I discovered that my first doctor was practising medicine in Quebec, breaking his legal undertaking in Ontario to suspend his practice until the appeal was decided on earlier charges to which he had pleaded guilty. The media was very interested in the three letters I had written to Augustin Roy, the president of the self-governing body for physicians in Quebec, who had given me the brush off when I alerted him to the predator he was sheltering. The ensuing battle between the Quebec government and Roy was spectacular; swarms of journalists planted themselves on the steps of Sacre Cœur Hospital in Montreal, where my doctor was employed.

The intensity of media attention was no doubt a factor in speeding up Quebec's disciplinary hearing, at which I testified. Around the same time, my doctor lost his appeal in Ontario, thus putting my case into abeyance; from then on I would function as a permanent deterrent to his reapplication to practise in the province. He also had his licence revoked in Quebec, but he had already left for Argentina, dislodged from practice by media attention where legal remedies had been inadequate.

It is sad that the media could speak louder and more emphatically than I could. Despite my personal vindication, I know that the media is *not* the best voice, should not be the voice we give this kind of authority to, because its attention is too fleeting, too shrill to be trusted with judgment. There is too great a margin of error. The media has gained this kind of influence because the legal system is failing us, moving too slowly, bound by archaic and byzantine rules. Ironically, the media and legal system have certain things in common. For both, voice becomes a generic reservoir of data that can be exploited and rearranged. There is no such thing as vision. Our voices as writers, our stories, specific and universal, that demand our and our readers' personal investment, are too often misused or denied their value. And the push is on politically to diminish us further, our voices like the whine of small wings that can be swept aside by a careless or calculating hand.

🌸 🌸

four landscapes

I

I told you about the landscape I crossed
since there in your office, last week,
you molested me.

My husband had aimed the nose of our car
out over the precipice, and we crossed
the Paugan Dam on one narrow track,
the river seeping high on our right
almost level with our wheels,
glassy and indifferent to us.
On our left, a drop of hundreds of feet,
chalky clenched rock of the river bottom
exposed, so bright it hurt my eyes,
too visible.

Our daughter in the back seat was edgy,
asking for reassurance,
as she had just given up her flying dreams
for dreams of falling,
the baby drowsed beside her in a milky cloud,
the white deposits of the cliffs
just like those on my shirts and sweaters.
My body was still giving, giving then,
and you wanted me to give more,
to give to you.

I told you about the migraine that flashed
as my heart raced across the narrow bridge,
above the unnatural drop,
the migraine that lasted all week,
and you said I led a very symbolic life,
that I lived inside one of my own poems
and wasn't it fascinating
how I had sought out a dam after our last
episode.

2

Symbol and psychosomatics having failed me,
I tried analogy.

I told you about the magazine article
I had just read in your tastefully decorated
waiting room, about the Pepsis wasp
that lives in your own fetid jungle,
your own treacherous homeland.
A wasp that lures and paralyses only one
of four hundred species of tarantula,
drags it to a pit it has carefully custom dug,
having taken measurements by crawling
harmlessly over the whole body,
like a tickle, a little insect tease,

and buries it alive with its egg sac
fastened to a bite-wound by poison and spit.
I told you with great feeling,
and perhaps a few tears, about the spider
slowly sucked dry by baby wasps
who burst out of sand bunkers
into a heartless sky humming in their own image,
leaving behind this unmarked grave.
You sighed, always one to feel sorry
for yourself, so dim in your office
I could not tell if your wide mouth stretched
into a slinky grin as you said,
Ah, patients. That sounds so familiar.

3

Hunting season,
and metaphors went zinging by bright
as steel, a dazzle of small hits
in the migraines that were constant then.

I told you about driving north to teach,
first snow skittering across the road,
across the windshield like disintegrating
vision. Then standing on the roadside
near Gracefield to clear my sight,
then taking the back road into the reserve,
around the blind curve that skids
into the gully, every few miles catching sight
of a small spot of searing red on the move,
filling the bush with pain.

I told you about pulling into a clearing
with a flimsy shed decorated with antlers,
where I paced shaky before the class
I couldn't fathom how I would stand through
let alone teach. *Porphyria's Lover*,
My Last Duchess lying duplicated
on the back seat of my car.

I shuddered all that fall, and stood
teetering alone as winter blew into a clearing
where two deer hung gutted above me.
I stood shrunken beneath the deers' spread legs,
red cavities ripped clean,
rib-cage and pelvis slit, plush and wide.
Obviously, you said, you're afraid
of how much you want to open to me.

4

This landscape speaks volumes
of water, 4000 cubic feet per second
plummeting 83 metres, almost twice the height
of Niagara Falls. Precision matters much
to me right now, as I have taken the vow
of truth, so much like the wedding vow,
nothing held back, *Do you promise to tell* ...
I do. I do. Strange how they swear you in,
but never swear you out, so that
the rest of your life is testimony.

After the trial, my husband and I
cross the catwalk above Chute Montmorency,
our children tight in our wake.
We all bend, hands gripping hoods, holding
each other against gusts of rain.
This is not a poem we walk through,
but raw physics. Not metaphor,
but slipping sliding beneath our feet,
and the women you swept over the edge
are struggling to surface, the suicides,
and the ones who never told a soul.
Their anger ionizes the mist, rings in my ears.

Landscape is not decor, was never anything
but this place we inhabit completely,
genuine cliffs with terrible drops,
fierce chill in the air, a man
hidden with a gun, who lay in sniper position
just beyond that desolate ring of trees
calculating whether I would stand or fall.

Silences longer than we can bear

JOHN BARTON

John Barton has published six books of poetry, including *Great Men* (Quarry Press), *Notes toward a Family Tree* (Quarry Press), *Designs from the Interior* (House of Anansi), *Sweet Ellipsis* (ECW Press), and *West of Darkness* (Penumbra Press). He lives in Ottawa, where he co-edits the poetry magazine *Arc*. His own poetry has been anthologized in *The Inner Ear, Reconcilable Differences, Garden Varieties*, and *Vintage 95*. Barton is a two-time winner of the Archibald Lampman Award, and a 1995 winner of the Ottawa-Carleton Book Award. He is also the recipient of the 1986 Patricia Hackett Award for Poetry from the University of Western Australia.

Silences longer than we can bear

❧ ❦

When I was in my late twenties I lost control of my life. While what happened is in itself of no importance here, suffice it to say I that felt so profoundly "life-threatened," I chose to inhabit the one refuge left where I had some power, my body. This outpost of bones, orifices, and soft tissue was mine to do with as I pleased, so I began to explore what I had long silenced in myself, my homosexuality. Given society's assumptions about the lives of gay men and lesbians, it might appear strange that I decided to face this nemesis when my life was already so complicated. But I felt that I had no choice but to choose. On 19 May 1969, then prime minister Trudeau decriminalized consensual sexual acts between adults of the same sex. Sixteen years later, I could, at minimum, close the bedroom door on my problems with the man of my choice.

In order to combat silence, we all must first combat the silences we impose on ourselves. During this time I began to read gay male fiction. Perhaps it is only appropriate that as a writer I should first look for myself in the public words of other writers further along in imagining a world where people such as ourselves exist. However, I had already written about my homosexuality several years before and, in fact, was about to publish some of this writing in my second book, *Hidden Structure*. This long poem explores the desire to love both men and women and is where I began to articulate and explore the nature of my sexuality. As it turned out, upon the book's completion, I fell in love with a woman, not a man. During the years that followed and before I faced my homosexuality once and for all, I wrote poems about heterosexual relationships.

Before and during the composition of *Hidden Structure,* I wrote other poems on gay themes. These languished in a file folder and were mostly forgotten. When I was finally out to myself, I began to revise, to re-hear these poems and read them aloud to others. Yet I had no confidence in them. Did other gay men feel as I felt? I remember showing one poem to a childhood friend who came out just before I did. Much to my amazement, he was moved and delighted. Through revealing something hidden, through breaking silence, I discovered a kinship based in sensibility and experience that had value to someone else.

All this leads me to what I want to talk to you about: how I came to publish *Great Men.* I explain in the book's acknowledgments that it "was written over ten years. It is a book that I had no idea I was writing, but not long ago I became aware of some kind of coherence hidden in the tumult." The important words here are "aware," "coherence," and "hidden," for they imply "vision," "identity," and "revelation." Also important is the phrase "I had no idea," for I believe self-awareness takes us by surprise, takes no prisoners. The book that I had planned to write was one where gay and straight were fused into a single vision, under the working title, *Comedians in the Same Desire.* This reconciliation was to elude me — pronoun agreements proved particularly contradictory — so I broke the manuscript in two. Each half took on a life of its own: one became *Great Men;* the other, *Notes toward a Family Tree,* is, among other things, my last heterosexual book and a fond and final farewell to straight sex. I decided not to silence one book in favor of the other.

My intention in *Great Men* was to show one example of how gay consciousness emerges and to share this experience not only with gay readers, but with straight ones as well. Timothy Findley, in his memoir, *Inside Memory,* states that the writer bears witness.[1] I wanted to be a witness not only to my life journey, but to similar journeys made by those like myself. I wanted straight audiences to realize that the desire to love and to be loved is the same need no matter how the bodies join. I wanted gay readers to see and have a positive vision of themselves and their destiny. The differences between gay men and lesbians and straight men and women lie less in how they make love and more in their socialization and politics. Gay socialization encourages us to be silent, our politics invoke us to speak, to protest, to be angry, to be ready, to be randy, to be joyous. Breaking silence is not an easy journey. When I emerged from my own silence, I thought that I only needed to open the door. I realize now that the door out is a tunnel. Its supports are the culture's belief that I should remain silent/celibate. If I insist on loving men, I should not talk, let alone write, about it, because I have nothing to be proud of. I have squandered my place in the patriarchy, have sacrificed my omnipotence, my potency, will never father sons. I have forsaken my responsibilities, for sons are the engines of the economy, are genetic RSPs. Because of this, the Mulroney government[2] refuses to honor its promise to amend the Canadian Human Rights Act in order to protect me and others from discrimination on the basis of whom I choose to sleep with. Because of this, in order to walk on the street at night, I must suppress any fear I have of being attacked as other men have been in Majors Hill Park within sight of the Peace Tower on Parliament Hill.

Nevertheless, according to Audré Lorde, the black lesbian poet, in her essay "The Transformation of Silence into Language and Action," our silences will not protect us. When we speak, she says, "it is never without fear — of visibility, of the harsh light of scrutiny, and perhaps judgment, of pain, of death. But [she continues] we have lived through all of those already, in silence, except death. And I remind myself all the time now that if I were to have been born mute, or had maintained an oath of silence my whole life long for safety, I would still have suffered, and I would still die." She also says, "for every real word spoken, for every attempt I had made to speak those truths for which I am still seeking, I had made contact."[3] For me, as a gay male writer, this is the essence of breaking silence: to connect, to say my story is part of the human story.

I want to share with you the response to *Great Men,* in the gay and the so-called mainstream press. The book is composed of three parts, the first and third of which are more politically engaged and explicitly gay, the second being composed of less polemical, more lyrical love poems where the genders of both the narrator and the person addressed are mostly implied. Gay critics tend to like the more overtly gay sections and dislike or are indifferent to the love poems. I find this reaction interesting. I chose to write the love poems in such a way that any reader, regardless of his or her sexual proclivities, would be able to identify with the impulse behind them, which is to love and be loved. The first and last sections of the book frame them and, therefore, cause the reader to view them as gay love poems. As an oppressed people, some gay men and lesbians look for very exacting mirrors of themselves in order to affirm their existence. Straight readers and critics have tended to focus more on the love poems. Is it because they are familiar and therefore safe? Or should I say safer?

In more recent work, I aim for more explicitness. In *Great Men*, I only rewrote one love poem, "Sustenance," in order to make its eroticism unambiguously gay and male. With this revision I crossed a line imaginatively that I would never re-cross, though I left the rest of the poems as they were written if only to justify, to render palatable, my flavor of love. I have no such need now, and if, to paraphrase Sylvia Plath, I want to "eat men like air,"[4] you'd better be prepared to eat them with me.

Only once, in any of the critical response to *Great Men*, did I feel any conscious or unconscious intent to silence me. In "Poets' Corner" in the April 1991 issue of *Books in Canada,* Maurice Mierau says mine is a coming-out story, but does not state what kind. Noting that I use lines from Cavafy as an epigraph, he sees my work as the product of "a Canadian voice that hasn't become too Greek for us to believe" — whatever that means. Nowhere in the review do I get a strong sense that this book is about gay love. It is implied, I admit; but as a gay person, I am sick of implication. Only until straights can be as open about us as gay people are about them will the issue of silence and silencing finally be put to rest.

I close with a stanza from one of my more recent poems, which I feel summarizes what I am trying to explore in my writing:[5]

We all carry a darkness inside us
that has nothing to do with
forest roads, cities, and moonless nights.
It is not what we are born to,
but it shadows forth within us
as we age, desire casting
silences longer than we can bear.
We all run before them, but must learn
to stop, learn to carry this darkness
toward each other with unblaming hands of light.

Notes

1. Timothy Findley, *Inside Memory: Pages from a Writer's Workbook* (Toronto: HarperCollins, 1990), p. 313.

2. This paper was presented in May 1992, seventeen months prior to the defeat of the Mulroney Conservatives in October 1993. In 1996, under much pressure, the Chretien Liberal government finally introduced legislation to create equality rights. The Bill passed May 9th in a controversial free vote in the House of Commons, controversial because it implies human rights are a matter of individual conscience rather than fundamental to Canadian society.

3. Audré Lorde, "The Transformation of Silence into Language and Action," in *Sister Outsider: Essays and Speeches* (Freedom, California: The Crossing Press, 1984), pp. 41, 43.

4. Sylvia Plath, "Lady Lazarus," in *Ariel* (London: Faber and Faber, 1965), p. 19.

5. "The Man from Grande Prairie," in *Designs from the Interior* (Concord, Ontario: House of Anansi, 1994), p. 106.

❧ ❦

Undercurrent

This is a bad semaphore
we practise
under the trees in the darkness, the damp white flags

of our t-shirts unable
to tease out

surrender as we move toward and away and past

one another, eyes
hungrily averted as we

pause

feet apart somewhere downstream along this
bridle path by the river,
the invisible

sibilant undercurrent deafened
by the cicada roar —
electric

morse code charging
the humid air of the city,
singing the *long, long, ecstatic short*

circuit of desire, the physiologic

imperative to be spent,
to be filled,

the white of our t-shirt dampness

impotent in the moonlight,
stained by pollen loose on the breeze,

what we want
not meant by the language

we tease out with flags,
its indefinite

pronouns not about the long
first person singulars of our cocks,
intimacy

straining against cotton shorts,
this language
the only language of love

available, though it does not include
us as *we*,
though we use it

badly, the damp t-shirt whiteness,
the fraternal tanned
presence underneath smelling of river algae and sweat

not drawing us closer,
our fear of how the white

flags of language distort

our kinship, seal us in the airless
eternal privacy of *they*

at the bottom of the river, graveyard of lovers

who unlike us, beloved stranger
(the park signs want us to believe)

could not resist the vortex.

Women and Violence: Another, Mother, Way

SUSAN MCMASTER

Susan McMaster is an Ottawa poet whose books include *Dark Galaxies*, *The Hummingbird Murders*, *Learning to Ride*, and *Uncommon Prayer: A Book of Dedications;* the anthology *Dangerous Graces: Women's Poetry on Stage* (ed.); and the wordmusic collections *Pass this way again*, *Wordmusic* (audiotape), and *North/South* (co-author). She was the founding editor of the feminist magazine *Branching Out* and an original member of the intermedia group First Draft. She has served as chair of the League of Canadian Poets' Freedom of Expression committee, coordinator of the Feminist Caucus, and editor of the Living Archives series. She performs with the music and poetry group *SugarBeat*. She has received the Canadian Authors Association and the Jane Jordan Awards. Her work has been anthologized in *Vintage 93*, *Celebrating Canadian Women*, and *A Room at the Heart of Things*.

Women and Violence: Another, Mother, Way

❧ ❦

I didn't want to write this piece. What could I say on the issue of women and violence? I didn't want to face the dark figures of my nightmares. I didn't want to pontificate on horrors that I — middle class, educated, healthy, happy — knew almost nothing of compared to the battered, the poor, new immigrants, native women, gay women . . .

Yet I couldn't refuse to speak, for I come from one of the historic peace churches — the Religious Society of Friends, or Quakers. The issue of violence and how to deal with it matters to me. It was always present in my household, in the myths that surrounded me as a child. I was raised to be a pacifist, a nonviolent activist, in a family that tried live within the Friends' principle of gender equality. I should have something to say on this subject. I should be a success story.

The feminist philosophy offers a utopian vision much like that held by Quakers. It's one that goes back to Mill, to Jesus, to the rabbinic sages, the Buddhas, Socrates — and to all the unrecorded women who shared and created these dreams. It's found today in the writings of the Brossards, the Mourés, the de Beauvoirs, and in the actions of every parent, teacher, or editor who shows someone how to use a hammer or an equation or an inclusive pronoun. It's a vision of education, a vision of right-thinking people working together towards a just and compassionate future. It comes down, at base, to the idea of raising our children right.

Easy to say. What does it mean in practical fact? For me, as a Quaker child, I learned that pacifism requires, not submission and "passivism," but an active commitment to *pacem facens* — to making peace. Truth, love, the light are one and the same, I came to believe, and there is "that of God in every one." I was taught that I had to get out there and *do* something, especially in the areas of politics and social concerns. Civil rights for Black Americans was the big issue when I was a young teenager; at the age of thirteen I tried to hitchhike south to join the protests. Later, there were anti-war demonstrations — remember "Ban the Bomb" and the Vietnam marches? I grew up during the Cold War: on almost all points I thought and acted differently from my school friends and teachers. I refused to stand for the anthem or "God Save the Queen" because nationalism fuels war and monarchism is anti-egalitarian. Remembrance Day was a nightmare, especially in those days, when all the rhetoric was about our brave boys, with little mention of the horrors of battle or concentration camps or Hiroshima. One can perhaps draw a parallel to a feminist working and living in many of today's environments, and trying, for example, to convince co-workers to wear a white ribbon to commemorate the fourteen female engineers killed because of their gender in Montreal.

At home, there was, theoretically at least a consciously nonviolent approach to discipline and sibling squabbles — which means that I remember a lot of "serious talks" and "cooling down sessions." At the time I sometimes thought a quick slap would be simpler; but now I have children of my own, I understand how frighteningly easy it is for one blow to escalate into an increasingly violent pattern, and I'm grateful for the restraint my parents showed and, more or less, taught me.

Again, the analogy here is to the new attitudes we as feminists are currently trying to teach our children and friends and selves, especially towards the issue of gender violence. It shows in the nonviolent conflict resolution methods we try to use, in our consensual approach to decision-making, in our efforts to speak out against societal wrongs and speak up for humanitarian values.

The Quaker theory is that positive peace-making, supported through universal education within a just society, and undertaken in a spirit of practical love and rational application, will produce a world in which occasions for violence tend to disappear.

Most feminist theory, as I understand it, says exactly the same thing: if we can educate people about what's wrong with patriarchal structures, establish a caring and egalitarian society, and raise our children in that context, sexism and the many the associated violences of racism, classism, economic discrimination, and so on will fade away.

Can it work?

As a young woman, I believed in the pacifist principles I was taught as intensely as any modern feminist believes now in gender equality. As an adult, I embraced the feminist movement with recognition and relief, started a feminist magazine, joined awareness groups and coops, worked for film-for-women projects, and participated in all the other ventures we explored in those early days. At last my marginal principles were becoming respectable; at last I was actually doing something to try and change my society.

And yet, often I felt like a monumentally failed Quaker.

And a monumentally failed feminist.

Somehow, looking back, they seem to go together.

Because, in spite of my training, I couldn't escape the effect of the values all around me. I remember how thoroughly I bought into society's obsession with male dominance, for example. One year, away from home for the first time, I read, I estimate, 250 Harlequin romances. Rape fantasies at times formed a far larger part of my mental world than I'd even now like to admit. (This, I think, happens to many of us at some point or other, but it's shameful, of course, something no-one likes to talk about.) Like many another idealist, I held one set of principles with my mind but couldn't train my emotions and actions to follow.

As a result, I found myself in predictable situations over and over again, attracted to harmful men on the one hand, lashing out irresponsibly and destructively on the other. As a teenager, I remember throwing my sister down the stairs. As a young mother I came a blackout short of battering my baby's head against the wall. As a supposedly mature adult, I played too often and stupidly with suicide, drowned my awareness in various toxins, turning cruelly and blindly against myself and those who loved me. All of these are patterns common in our society, violent and primitive reactions to stresses and distortions too pervasive and familiar to need naming.

(For years I looked for the source of all this in my private life, probing into dark areas, losses of memory, recurring nightmares . . . More and more nowadays I wonder how much comes from weaknesses in the society we live in, projecting themselves through my instincts and dreams. Writing poetry is one way I ask this question.)

That is one side of the story. And yet, there is another. Some of my childhood training took, and overrode my submission to the world around. Often, without even being aware of it, I find myself acting in ways that spring directly from my learned, optimistic belief in that of

God in every one, find myself using the practical techniques of nonviolence and constructive conflict resolution I'd been taught.

I remember talking myself out of danger in rough situations many times — usually by asking my attacker's name as a starting point. I remember moving without fear and therefore safely as a youth through a seventies world of drug dealers and motorcycle gangs. I remember walking downtown streets at four in the morning without harm. I've been lucky in my friendships, in the ease I feel with co-workers, in my positive interactions with acquaintances and strangers alike. In spite of my romantic idiocies, in the end I married a gentle man.

Slowly, as I've grown older and less frantic, I've found ways to act more effectively upon the principles I believe in. The groups I've helped organize — for example, two intermedia performance groups, a woman's magazine, various publishing ventures, literary and community projects, union activities — tend to operate using Quaker methods of consensus and shared responsibility; negotiation and practical conflict resolution are areas where I find it easy to contribute.

How to make sense of this mixture? Can I see any causal relationships in the pattern of my life, or am I simply floating on the sea of the random bad and good luck we all have? Has my early training in peacemaking led to any noticeable result? If so, am I justified in suggesting one life offers an example of a chance of real change, even inside a society which still operates on older, more vicious principles?

And so my qualms when asked to address the question of women and violence. On what ground should I stand? From where can I speak? How, as a working poet, can I formulate these questions in a way that will mean something to my readers, will mean something in the larger world we inhabit? Writing this essay has forced me into contemplation of this conundrum.

And I find a glimmer of hope.

First, let me dispose of the negatives. No, I do not believe in any easy utopias. The United Nations has not abolished war; technology has not eliminated hunger; the franchise has not ended corrupt government. Nor will education of our children or ourselves totally transform the world and end violence among societies, between men and women, by parents against children, by ourselves against ourselves. Art, music, poetry, far from being panaceas, are all too often a submissive repetition of the darkest and most unacknowledged, unvoiced urges we carry inside our childish and frightened nightmares. Even poetry that speaks so it can be heard, that learns to "speak truth to power," in the old Quaker phrase, is no more than a whisper in a gale.

But yes, I do believe change is possible. Both the events of the larger world and my own life have forced me into an understanding of the human skin and bones and guts of us all. Into an acceptance of the terrible resources for hate and violence and abuse of power that are part of being human. This recognition requires me to look for ways of resolving and preventing such horrors that do not set me outside of, or above, any *other*. For though I believe we are all potentially imbued with God, no one person or religion or philosophy seems to me to be uniquely privy to any ultimate "truth." We are all seekers, all afraid and alone. The belief, taught to me in my cradle, that as well as the dark we all share something of "the light," gives me a way to forgive myself, which is the root and true dynamic of peace-making.

Similarly, my parents' example means I easily apply such methods in my own parenting. I don't use corporal discipline. I try to treat my children as equal in status in our community of family. I look for non-destructive ways to help them deal with anger and pain. And my children seem, as a result — uncross my fingers O Witch Mother! — so much less troubled than we were. (Maybe one of them will reply to this paper in twenty years and call me wrong . . . .)

Looking beyond myself, I'm encouraged that feminists, like Quakers, believe in education and act on that belief. This anthology is one example. Another is the many feminist study courses now available in universities and high schools. At the same time, pacifist principles and techniques — what we today call conflict resolution, consensual decision-making, and mediation skills — are being researched in places like the Canadian Peace Institute and applied by groups like the Peace Brigades.

Beyond education, what will change things? Not force — prisons and punishments and revenge. These are temporary palliatives (if such they are), no more effective in the long run than the Great War was in ending all wars, or the Final Solution in eradicating strife between Gentiles and Jews. All forms of destructive control, from economic and physical to the ultimate dehumanization of indifference and suicide, are forms of violence. And any victim of violence has an utopian vision. If there is room for nothing but anger, then this vision is one of destruction. Thus we have the wife murdering her battering husband, cousins blowing up cousins in Ireland, the South African necklacing a neighbor.

In the story of the good guys and the bad guys someone has to win — and someone has to die.

But that is not a woman's story. In her story, the man attacking her is the husband she sometimes loves, the uncle she trusted, the son she nurtured. She cannot make a happy ending by destroying him. (We have the related fallacy that a good woman can reform a bad man — also a simplistic story with no happy ending.) In a woman's story, it is her own fear that makes her turn away, ignore the harm being done to her children. No true woman's story — or real human story — has an ending in which force vanquishes evil. Rather, her story must be one that allows for complexity, change, a possible future. She must, in fact, be a peace-maker.

My mother, whose words accompany me throughout my life, says, learn to forgive, for you become what you hate.

As a poet, I maintain that really noticing something, naming it, is the positive, first, and necessary step towards changing it. It is the essential element in education. The poem may be despairing or even brutal, but as long as it tells the truth, it allows the possibility of transformation. No-one can strike down a new path with her or his eyes closed. I seldom march or demonstrate anymore, my poetry is anything but overtly political, but I do my best to tell what I see, as I see it, in every grimy or delightful detail. I believe that writing about our state of humanness, paying attention with words in such a way that the importance of each person becomes clear, calling into question the assumptions we run with — I believe this is worthwhile, may even change an individual or society for the better. My poetry is informed (and, of course, limited) by what I've learned through my life about sociology and physics and history and literature and feminism, and most especially about peace-making; I hope it presents a way of looking at the world which offers the possibility of resolution and compassion. I hope it offers a vision of caring. A vision of a world in which the loving education of our children in practical, creative peace-making can indeed lead to a new, more humane society where acts of gender violence, or economic or cultural violence, or violence of any kind at all are viewed with disgust and horror, instead of the veiled approval they often receive today.

This is true pacifism, the only effective, long-term answer to violence. This is, I believe, the most fruitful feminist vision, the one for which I am willing to work. There may be no Utopia. But there may be a way to change our society for the better. Another, mother, way.

Ambush

You get ambushed from the side
sometimes
a fine life, a quiet day
and suddenly
you're shaking at the hip
with tremors from some
forgotten waste
some iced-over scree
that cracks without warning
shudders, breaks

and no time to fix anything —
no time, no way —

You tell me, sure
I won't believe
your secret tale

I gather my heart
fold shock tight inside
as I fold you in
I believe you, I say
How could I not?

And weeks and weeks later
among different stories
in another place

a sudden split —
I start to shake —

stumble through days
on a slope of shale
that could tumble, slip
at a whisper
expose
the black mouth
of a yawning cave

I listen to the click
of falling stone

listen and shake

Silence(?)(! (.)

DANIEL DAVID MOSES

Poet and playwright Daniel David Moses is a Delaware from the Six Nations lands along the Grand River in southern-western Ontario. He lives in Toronto, where he writes full time and works with Native and cross-cultural arts organizations. His poetry is collected in *Delicate Bodies* (Blewointment/ Nightwood) and *The White Line* (Fifth House). His plays include *Coyote City*, *Almighty Voice and His Wife*, *Big Buck City*, *Brébeuf's Ghost*, and the prize-winning one-act plays *The Dreaming Beauty* and *The Moon and Dead Indians*. The last play, with its companion piece, *Angel of the Medicine Show*, has been produced by Théâtre Passe Muraille and published by Exile Editions as *The Indian Medicine Shows*. He was a finalist for the Governor General's Award for Drama in 1991, won first prize in the Canadian National Playwrighting Competition, and the James Buller Memorial Award for Excellence in Aboriginal Theatre. He is also co-editor with Terry Goldie of *An Anthology of Canadian Native Literature in English* (Oxford University Press, 1992). His own work has been anthologized in, among others, *Returning the Gift: Poetry and Prose from the First North American Native Writers' Festival* and *Borderlines*.

Silence (?) (!) (.)

❦ ❦

My first thoughts on receiving the request that I take part in a panel on Silence had to do with that part of language which languishes, unstudied but mysterious, between the period we place at the end of one sentence and the capital letter we use to start the next.

You know, that space on the page that allows us, in reading, a moment for the lungs and the mind to inspire — to take in the spirit of our subject matter (which means, of course, that the other parts of a sentence — let's call them words — connect with expiring, not only in the last sigh sense that most obviously lies in the period, but also in the sense of getting the spirit of our subject matter out of our minds and into the air or onto the page).

I mean silences: blanks, places of nullity or neutrality, that were, if you can imagine it, my big discovery as an undergraduate. Talk about belaboring the obvious. Rests in music, clear color in paintings, stillness in dance, silence in drama and poetry. Form versus content turned in my mind from a dichotomy, a conflict, an argument — all concepts I was unconsciously but nevertheless profoundly uncomfortable with in those school years, concepts that were very much central to what I was supposed to be learning to accept — into a process, a tension, a vividness, a constant shifting from foreground to background and back, a strobing from positive to negative, a concretion, a concatenation of sense. I'd found myself a little pearl of wisdom. Take a pause, take a breath, take a silence.

And much later I realized I was searching for an aesthetic that fit in with the way I'd been brought up. I mean, for instance, that we are taught in mainstream aesthetics that conflict is a necessary characteristic of drama. I had difficulty dealing with this because at home we were taught not to fight. How was I supposed to write a play if I thought conflict was more a failure of imagination than an adequate expression of emotion? I now use a different qualification for perhaps the same sorts of situations: I write plays full of contrast.

And what better contrast than that between words and silence?

These, more or less, were my first thoughts on silence.

Then I got the letter to confirm the panel and a requested paper — not a poem. Was that supposed to be an example of genre silencing? I wasn't sure I understood the intent of the accompanying suggested topics. Gender identity, color, genre, myth. *Am I blue? Aren't these tears in my eyes telling you?* I don't normally spend time as an essayist. Whose jargon is this anyway? Then I realized that what was wanted was Native politics or history, that I was supposed to be a representative of Canada's First Nations, that I was — not again! — the liberal's token Indian.

Hey, who elected me Chief?

As I said above, we're taught not to fight, we do not value conflict, and though I dislike feeding into any discussion of race (from my perspective our differences are in our cultures, thank you very much), I decided I would try to think again:

Indian culture? What do you want to know about that for? It won't do you any good.

My grandmother, my father's mother, who died last October at the age of ninety five, said that to me, way back years ago when she was much alive, when she was a lady and I myself was little more than a child.

A woman who spent her last years lying in bed, drifting toward death, losing flesh as if it were her memory, growing small — but not like a child.

On a typical visit, I'd say: Do you know who I am?

And after a moment, she'd say, Oh yes.
Who?

Silence.

Had she forgotten?

Or could she have been withholding her words, like a child whose only power lies in refusal?

It won't do you any good.

And I thought, no, I don't want to talk about Indian this or that. I thought that my grandmother was right about Indian culture, at least if it's the history and politics of race and property and pain. Owning that will gain me nothing.

So if you want it, here, I give it to you. Not that it's really mine to give. That story's yours, certainly. You who can choose to put me in this position. Maybe Indian culture will someday belong to all of us, be ours. But some owning up to it needs to be done first.

And there were other thoughts having to do with silence and the experience of it, ideas both social and aesthetic, ideas autobiographical and personally political. But they belong to some Delaware from the Six Nations lands who realizes now that this is not the place for them and that he's come as far along the backtrack as he can.

Do you know who I am? he asks.

Who?

The Ends of a Picnic

Oh you're black and lucky, bird, strutting through the grass
out into the sun — and away from an impasse
in conversation, from words gone blue, too sour
in the heat, ever to chew on, let alone eat.

We could be lucky too or bright with a slew of
picnic fixings to squeeze into our beaks in lieu.
How nice to have pre-sliced cheese and cold cuts to share,
I've always said. How nice to break bread. You don't need

knives to – and chance is with us, since we did forget
to bring a blade along into the shade today
where the green of lawns won't be cutting off any
arteries. Wit's evident too in these far too

few sweet grapes included on the menu. Or is
that irony one only I have the taste for?
We're sharing the relative calm of a blanket
spread out in the public sun but the appetites,

yes, the vocabulary, we held in common
are gone or in need of translation. Is that why
you're here, you dark and winged thing, to bring some sense
back into our heads, our sentences? To feed off

all the clever words we said? To take them up through
the haze of poplar fluff and leave the silences
we're waiting in as white as the face of the pond is
under a cover of the stuff? No reflections

show up there or here unless the wind or we stir
— and who dares at these temperatures? Only you
and the one young man who strutted over the grass
too, cocky as you, as the red and yellow off

your wings. He's made the trek all the way uphill out
of the shade and now, bending over the spouting
fountain there, like the sun licking at his brown skin
for bright sweat, he begins sucking up, sucking at

that jet as if it really were a spring, really
that sort of first ever clear flowing, like the one
that got the two of us going, somehow made us
unafraid to go along on this escapade.

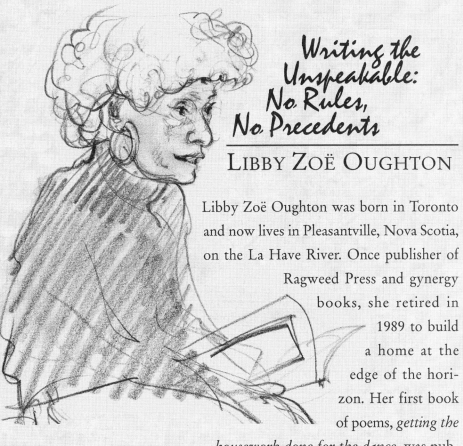

Writing the Unspeakable: No Rules, No Precedents

LIBBY ZOË OUGHTON

Libby Zoë Oughton was born in Toronto and now lives in Pleasantville, Nova Scotia, on the La Have River. Once publisher of Ragweed Press and gynergy books, she retired in 1989 to build a home at the edge of the horizon. Her first book of poems, *getting the housework done for the dance*, was published in 1988. A short story won the Carl Sentner Literary Award in Prince Edward Island and also appeared in the anthology *Frictions: Stories by Women* (Second Story Press). Recently she has become interested in Buddhism, and is the co-editor of *Ayurvedic Cooking for Self-Healing*.

Writing the Unspeakable: No Rules, No Precedents

※ ※

In 1987, the old building that housed Ragweed Press was torched by an arsonist. As the owner and dreamer, I was heartbroken to see seven years of work charred and sodden around me, and just at a time when I had decided to concentrate on publishing poetry and prose by women. I wasn't sure that we could ever clean up the mess and get back on track. Shortly after the fire, I decided to honor a commitment I had made to myself: attend the women's writing school at WestWord, as a student, and get away for a while.

Nicole Brossard was teaching fiction that year. I'd barely walked in the door when she grabbed my arm, saying that one of the students in her group had submitted a manuscript that must be published. I remember thinking that a new manuscript was about the last thing I needed. I didn't even have an office, let alone a chair to sit down. But as she talked about it, I caught her excitement, and wonder, and agreed to read it as soon as I had time.

Before I had that time, I heard the author read from the manuscript — a scared, quiet, monotone voice filled my ears and tore away at my heart. I heard content and a language I had never, ever heard before. And I was stunned. I knew in my belly that it must be published. The author was Elly Danica, and the manuscript, untitled back then, was about incest. It was written like machine-gun fire — deceptively simple words and short sentences carried the incredible power of a devastating story.

Elly, Nicole, and I talked long hours in the University of British

Columbia's School of Theology about just how we should go about publishing it. Elly wasn't sure she wanted it published at all, because even though she hadn't mentioned them by name, the people in her story were still alive. Elly herself was extremely fragile. Attending the writing school was the first time in thirteen years of healing herself that she had been out into the larger world. She lived in a small church in the prairies. The world was a terrifying place for her.

With Nicole's help, Elly agreed to have the manuscript published, as long as we kept it absolutely secret — no publicity, no catalogue listing, no author tours, nothing. I agreed, despite knowing this was not a particularly wise move economically for a small regional publisher. I also agreed to get it into print in less than a year, when I didn't know whether I had even the backbone of a publishing house left.

I also agreed to attempt the editing. I returned to Prince Edward Island, and Elly sent the manuscript within the month. I then began the hardest editing work I have ever done — not in terms of quantity, but in sheer emotional response. I was so utterly angry about each word on the page, wanting to use my red pen as a weapon. Throughout the editing, design, and production, Elly needed a great deal of support. Many times she threatened to tear up the manuscript, or tear herself up. She couldn't look at any of the editing and she was paranoid about seeing the book in print. It was a hair-raising time: trying to glue the press back together so it could begin functioning again; trying to keep Elly somewhat sane and calm by long distance; and constantly reassuring her that she would never be forced to appear in public.

I believed so much in the work that I simply did whatever I could to help the book and Elly along. I doubt that many publishers would have taken all the midnight phone calls and anything else that was required. But at that time it seemed part of the whole urgent process of helping women to be heard, of women writing words, writing their lives, writing the unspeakable, lifting the pressure cooker lid of silence.

The book, entitled *DON'T: A Woman's Word,* came out in May 1988, a scant eight months after I'd received the manuscript. Elly agreed to a small launching at the SCM bookstore in Toronto and to attend the Feminist Book Fair, held in Montreal that year. At the fair we made contacts that resulted in German, British, American, and Irish editions, but the book slept in Canada. This was partly because Sylvia Fraser's book *My Father's House: A Memoir of Incest and of Healing* was much in the floodlights, and especially because *DON'T* was published by a small regional press under a new feminist label: gynergy. It wasn't until a friend of Elly's personally gave Peter Gzowski a copy and he decided to visit Elly in the church and do a major "Morningside" interview with Elly that the floodgates opened. CBC phone lines were jammed, we were overwhelmed, and suddenly everyone wanted in on the act. All of this had to be carefully screened to shield Elly. The radio program brought us a flood of "abuse" manuscripts, phone calls, and late night knocks on the door from women who needed help. It was clear we were becoming known as a "sympathetic haven" for women who needed to tell their stories. My staff and I could barely cope with the effect of one book, let alone this.

Within a year the book had sold well over 15,000 copies and come out in mass market paperback. Elly had begun travelling the country giving readings and workshops and doing what she always dreamed of but never imagined possible — using the book to raise real consciousness about the issue of incest and abuse.

Although Ragweed/gynergy is no longer in my life, Elly Danica very much is. The mass market edition of *DON'T* is long out of print, though the gynergy edition survives. Elly's book is taught on many, many feminist study courses across Canada, and scholarly papers and articles continue to be written about it. Her phone, her mailbox, and even her doorstep in the prairie village still bring the words, the cries of women in desperate need. When Elly is feeling strong, she tries to help. (This in itself is almost a full-time job, she has commented.) But this does not pay the bills or put food on her table. Often Elly does not know where her next meal is coming from. She is not able to work at this or that out in the world, as most of us can. She wants, simply, to write — to write beyond *DON'T* — a mistress of spare and powerful words, not to be stuck in a lifetime of "victim" roles, either writing or lecturing or . . .

But the daily act of basic living is so tenuous for Elly that she finds little peace in which to write. She has three novels underway in various early stages, and is currently trying to complete the *DON'T* sequel, about everything the book has wrought in her life, in other lives. (As she said a few days ago on the phone, tongue-in-cheek, *DON'T, Too*).

Elly's dream is to leave the prairies, the scene, and move east to the sea. For her, the silence has changed color, but still remains.

I have told you this story as an example of one kind of feminist publishing in order to suggest that women's words are so vital that there are no rules, no precedents for the form they may take. Neither are there any precedents, from my point of view as a publisher, as to what might be necessary to support and care for the author. For there is no separation of the feelings of the woman inside me from the pain and sheer courage of what Elly, or any other woman, might be writing about. It is, must continue to be, an integrated journey for both, for all of us, toward the light.

Postscript

Recently Libby Zoë Oughton became interested in an ancient Indian natural medicine called Ayurveda. She studied this for a year in New Mexico, and stayed for a second year to edit the book *Ayurvedic Cooking for Self Healing* (1992–94). While there, her horizon home in Prince Edward Island burnt down, taking everything — "every poem, every draft, my next two manuscripts, works in progress, art works, etc. . . . I haven't been able to write since — not a word . . . A fireblock. Where do the words go?" So, "being light and unattached," she travelled far and long through Greece, Turkey, India, and Nepal. She returned in 1995 to find a new home in Nova Scotia, and here, with her partner Dian, she lives and dreams, practising natural medicine, becoming a herbalist of local herbs, and being an artist and sculptor, especially in wood. "When all the ideas, urges, passions, wisdoms that lead to the poem, the story rise up, I pick up my carving knife and chisels and fashion something out of wood. Or draw. Or . . . anything but write. I feel very far from the world of writing and publishing these days." Her other "new and exciting journey" is a growing interest in and practise of Buddhism.

⊰❁ ❁⊱

woman/tongue

her cane   ageless stick of olive
drumming up my marble stairs
taptap steady shuffle rest and step
it is my neighbour Kassandra
coming for her morning visit always
after the mailtruck brings a letter
she draws   slowly from her great
black-shrouded motherbreast
to the intimate village landscape
of her apron calling
                    Ella! ELLA!
                    Aftō enai grāmma!

we are to translate this letter
Kassandra and i (who know but english)
from her visitor last summer (german)
for Kassandra (who speaks but greek)
and writes in none at all

first we discuss
the pretty coloured picture on the card
why! it's mary joseph and the
kookla! kookla! she begins
to rock the baby jesus to her breast
and look! there's heehaw meow woofwoof
bif BAAA and little baaa
                            she stops
rocking all the children of the world
not the least impressed by my english baaa
and launches into a much superior
lamb than i

next we read the words
inscribed inside (that I don't know)
which i translate into english and
Kassandra hears with utter satisfaction
nai she beams and nods *nai nai*
clasping my hand in hers
and we women roar with laughter
at the ruse   we do   we do

HEATHER SPEARS

Heather Spears' poetry collection *The Word for Sand* won the 1989 Governor General's Award for Poetry as well as the Pat Lowther Award, also given to *How to Read Faces* (1986). *Human Acts* (1991) won the CBC Literary Competition first prize for poetry. Books of her drawings and poetry include *Drawings from the Newborn* (1986), *Drawn from the Fire* (1989), and *Massacre* (1990). Recent publications are *The Panum Poems* (1996) and a Tesseracts science fiction trilogy.

MARIE ELYSE ST. GEORGE

Marie Elyse St. George collaborated with poet Anne Szumigalski on the book *Voices,* which won the 1996 Governor General's Award for Poetry. *Voices* collects works from an exhibition with Szumigalski at the Susan Whitney Gallery, Regina, in 1993, which culminated in a major exhibition at the Mendel Art Gallery, Saskatoon, in 1995. Born in Ontario and resident in Saskatchewan for twenty years, St. George has published and exhibited as a poet and artist in Canada, England, and the United States. Her book of poetry and art, *White Lions in the Afternoon,* was published by Coteau in 1987. In 1989, she won both the League of Canadian Poets National Poetry Prize and the Saskatchewan Writers Guild Prize.

LIVING ARCHIVES SERIES

Living Archives Series from the Feminist Caucus of the League of Canadian Poets:

Stats, Memos, and Memory, Cathy Ford and Sharon H. Nelson, edited and introduced by Cathy Ford (1982).

Two Women Talking: Correspondence 1985–87, Erin Mouré and Bronwen Wallace, Erin Mouré and Bronwen Wallace, edited and introduced by Susan McMaster (1985–87).

Illegitimate Positions: Women and Language, Margaret Christakos, Penn Kemp, Erin Mouré, Suniti Namjoshi, Lola Lemire Tostevin, Bronwen Wallace, edited and introduced by Susan McMaster (1987).

What Is a Nice Feminist. . .?, Di Brandt, Afua Cooper, Cathy Ford, Libby Zoë Oughton, Libby Scheier, Janice Williamson, edited and introduced by Sandra Nicholls (1989).

Women and Violence, Maja Bannerman, Di Brandt, Nadine McInnis, Susan McMaster, Brenda Niskala, edited and introduced by Sarah Klassen (1992).

Silences, John Barton, Ayanna Black, Richard Harrison, Penn Kemp, Daniel David Moses, Erin Mouré, edited and introduced by John Barton (1992).

Reinventing Memory, Marilyn Bowering, Neile Graham, Maria Jacobs, Sarah Klassen, Anne Szumigalski, Carolyn Zonailo, edited and introduced by Anne Burke (1993).

Belles lettres / beautiful letters, Anne Burke, Fred Cogswell, Magie Dominic, Heather Spears, edited by John Barton, introduced by Magie Dominic (1994).

Urban/Rural: Women, writing & place, Maja Bannerman, Kathy Fretwell, Marvyne Jenoff, Louise Halfe Sky Dancer, Neile Graham (1995), edited by Maja Bannerman.

Living Archives is an ongoing series; for subscription information or to purchase individual chapbooks, please contact the League of Canadian Poets, 54 Wolesely Street, Third Floor, Toronto, Ontario, Canada M5T 1A5, Telephone (416) 504-1657, Fax 703-0059, E-mail: league@io.org

Quarry Women's, Gay & Lesbian Books

Bronwen Wallace, *Arguments with the World*, ed. Joanne Page. $18.95 CDA/USA $14.95

Susan McMaster, *The Hummingbird Murders*. $14.95 CDA/USA $10.95

Susan McMaster, *Learning To Ride*. $14.95 CDA/USA $10.95

Susan McMaster, *Uncommon Prayer*. $14.95 CDA/USA $10.95

Susan McMaster, ed. *No More Dragons: Feminist Fantasies, Fables & Folktales*. $18.95 CDA/USA $12.95

Sandra Nichols, *Woman of Sticks, Woman of Stones*. $14.95 CDA/USA $10.95

Sandra Nichols, *The Untidy Bride*. $14.95 CDA/USA $10.95

Nadine McInnis, *The Litmus Body*. $14.95 CDA/USA $10.95

John Barton, *Great Men*. $14.95 CDA/USA $10.95

John Barton, *Notes Toward a Family Tree*. $14.95 CDA/USA $10.95

Elizabeth Smart, *Autobiographies*. $19.95 CDA/USA $14.95

Mira Markovic, *Night & Day*. $24.95 CDA/USA $16.95

Vivian Marple, *I Mention the Garden for Clarity* $14.95 CDA/USA $10.95

Maggie Helwig, *Eating Glass*. $14.95 CDA/USA $10.95

Dacia Maraini, *Traveling in the Gait of a Fox*. $14.95 CDA/USA $10.95

Genni Gunn, *Mating in Captivity*. $14.95 CDA/USA $10.95

Sarah Klassen, *Dangerous Elements*. $14.95 CDA/USA $10.95

Available at your favorite bookstore or directly from the publisher:
Quarry Press, P.O. Box 1061, Kingston, ON K7L 4Y5, Canada.
Tel. (613) 548-8429, Fax. (613) 548-1556, E-mail: order@quarrypress.com.

Name _____

Address _____

_____ Postal Code _____ Telephone _____

Visa/Mastercard# _____ Expiry Date _____

Signature _____

Your books will be shipped with an invoice
enclosed, including shipping costs, payable
within 30 days in Canadian or American currency
(credit card, check, or money order).